SELF-CO

SELF-DEVELOPMENT

SELF-COUNSELLING

How to develop the skills to positively manage your life

William Stewart

RIGHT, LET'S TALK ABOUT ME!

How To Books

By the same author:

Building Self-Esteem
Controlling Anxiety
Learning to Counsel (with Jan Sutton)

Cartoons by Mike Flanagan

British Library Cataloguing in Publication Data
A catalogue record for this book is available from the British Library.

First published in 1998 by How To Books Ltd, 3 Newtec Place,
Magdalen Road, Oxford, OX4 1RE, United Kingdom.
Tel: (01865) 793806. Fax: (01865) 248780.

Note: The material contained in this book is set out in good faith for
general guidance and no liability can be accepted for loss or expense
incurred as a result of relying in particular circumstances on statements
made in this book. The law and regulations may be complex and liable to
change, and readers should check the current position with the relevant
authorities before making personal arrangements.

Produced for How To Books by Deer Park Productions.
Typeset by Concept Communications (Design & Print) Ltd, Crayford, Kent.
Printed and bound by Cromwell Press, Trowbridge, Wiltshire.

Contents

List of Illustrations

Preface

The aim of this book is to help readers understand themselves better, and to be able to live richer and more fulfilled lives. I see this book as being an adjunct, not necessarily an alternative (although it may be for some), to face-to-face counselling.

This book takes counselling from a partnership with someone else, to a partnership with self. The inference that can be drawn by readers is that they can do something for themselves. Students on counselling courses would benefit from working through the book. People already in counselling or other forms of therapy would find that their insights are enhanced, and they are able to enter into a more active partnership with the trainer, therapist or counsellor.

More people are being drawn towards counselling, either as counsellors or as clients. A parallel can be drawn between this burgeoning of counselling and what happened at the start of the 20th century with the great surge forward of Neo-Freudian psychotherapists, based on Freud's psychoanalysis, many of them not subscribing to Freud's rigid interpretations, yet each contributing new insights to the body of knowledge of psychotherapy.

Carl Rogers, trained in psychoanalysis, brought fresh insights as he moved the process from being therapist-centred, with set interpretations, to client-centred counselling. Much of the mystique was removed, as it became feasible for 'ordinary' people to learn to be counsellors. At the same time Rogers, and his followers, stressed that person-centred counselling was not psychoanalysis, even though the insights certainly draw from it, as well as from other psychological therapies.

Finally, as many authors and therapists have said, clients are generally seen for a few hours weekly (as in psychoanalysis) or once a week (as in counselling); what happens within the client in the remaining hours – waking or sleeping? Whatever style of therapy (counselling), therapists would agree that more goes on within the client in the hours away from the consultation room than in it. The one hour a week is but a catalyst; it is up to the client to continue the work. Some do, others are so caught up in their difficulties that they (consciously) do little work by themselves.

This book could be given by counsellors to clients to continue the work and keep up the momentum. The more insights and skills clients can develop, the further client and counsellor will be able to travel along the road towards healing. But in the end, it is the client who is the principal actor; the counsellor is the facilitator. This book encourages the reader to be his or her own facilitator.

William Stewart

1
Exploring the Feasibility
of Self-Counselling

In her introduction to *Self-Analysis* (1942 and reissued in 1994), Karen Horney says: 'To an increasing degree people turn to analysis not because they suffer from depressions, phobias or comparable disorders but because they feel they cannot cope with life or feel that factors within themselves are holding them back or injuring their relationships with others.' Written over 50 years ago, this applies with even more force to the rapid development of counselling, and the awareness that counselling can help people to live life more effectively.

IDENTIFYING WHO BENEFITS FROM SELF-COUNSELLING

Self-counselling:

● helps people develop their self-awareness to deal with their own problems

● is a backup for people already in counselling

● can benefit students on counselling courses

● is cheaper than therapy.

COMPARING AND CONTRASTING PSYCHOANALYSIS AND COUNSELLING

While counselling draws on the insights derived from psychoanalysis, the two disciplines are different. Psychoanalysis deals more with people who are troubled by some deep-seated problem which often carries the label of neurosis. Counselling deals more with people whose emotional equilibrium is temporarily disturbed because of some difficulty with which they find it hard to cope. The 'more' is important, for many counsellors work at a level which goes beyond 'temporarily disturbed'.

The main purpose of psychoanalysis is to make unconscious material conscious. Psychoanalytical belief is that neuroses are acquired only during early childhood. Thus the *principal focus* is in the past, and the first few years of life; in counselling the *principal focus* is the present. The aim of both is to help the person to move forward.

This does not mean that psychoanalysis ignores the present and the future, and that counselling does not involve the past, but it is the principal focus which is different. In fact, it is impossible to look at the present without considering the past; to try to do so would be like trying to separate the white of an egg from the yolk. It can be done but one is left with something incomplete.

A basic assumption common to both psychoanalysis and counselling is that when we experience emotional conflict, to the extent that it interferes with daily living, we cease to live effectively; are incapable of enjoyment; and need to do something to resolve the conflict.

Defining the differences between psychoanalysis and counselling

Psychoanalysis deals more with people who are deeply troubled by some deep-seated problem which often carries the label of neurosis. Counselling deals more with people whose emotional equilibrium is temporarily disturbed because of some difficulty with which they find it hard to cope. In psychoanalysis the *principal focus* is in the past, and the first few years of life; in counselling the *principal focus* is the present.

EXPLORING THE FEASIBILITY OF BEING YOUR OWN COUNSELLOR

This brief excursion into what psychoanalysis is, and its similarities to and differences from counselling, paves the way for a more detailed discussion of how feasible it is to be one's own counsellor. Half a century ago it was assumed that analysis was *the* only reliable method to achieve personality growth. That this is not so hardly needs to be stated for counselling, any more than for psychoanalysis. Many other avenues have the potential for personal growth, including involvement in religion, work, a worthwhile interest, a loving relationship.

Understanding the demands

Being your own counsellor is not an easy option, for it can be every bit as demanding as face-to-face counselling. In reality, it can be more demanding. In self-counselling, the 'session' does not end; the door does not close. You find yourself being, as it were, the counsellor on your own shoulder, constantly pushing yourself, bringing something fresh to your mind, even waking you up in the middle of the night with a fresh insight.

Effective counselling hinges on a co-operative partnership between counsellor and client; without this co-operation little will be accomplished. Co-operation does not mean polite compliance, or agreeing with everything the counsellor proposes; nor does it mean simply giving information. Co-operation means entering into the exploration - fully. It does not mean being led by the hand; it often means going into the unknown, going where you have never gone before. That is counselling. That is self-counselling, too. The phrase 'test the water' is apt in counselling; and as we shall see, it should be the watchword in self-counselling.

Developing insights

Counsellors impart skills to their clients, and help them develop insights. It is important to distinguish 'help them to develop insights' from 'give insights.' Insights are highly personal, and cannot be 'given' by one person to another. I may tell the client that such and such brought insight to me, but that is as far as it can go. Insights must come fresh like the Eureka experience came to Archimedes in the bath, when he discovered the phenomenon of water displacement.

Nothing is more thrilling than when an insight dawns. It may have lingered for days or weeks, gradually working away in the subconscious, even figuring in your dreams, or with little flashes of sub-insights - something like looking through frosted glass. There the vision is dimmed; the form can be distinguished, but lacks detail. Thus with some insight. Not all come like bolts from the blue.

Sharing your insights - or not

Sharing insights has to be treated with caution. There might be a natural tendency to repeat the action of Archimedes, who, it is alleged, jumped out of the bath and ran down the street naked, telling the astonished inhabitants of Syracuse, 'I have found it!' No doubt the startled populace laughed at Archimedes' insight; people might not laugh at yours, but they might not appreciate what it means to you, and that is much the same thing. So, treat your insights with the greatest respect, and share them only when you have absorbed them into your innermost being, and when they have taken root, and produced good fruit. Even then, be careful with whom you share. Don't, as the Bible says, cast your pearls before swine.

Coping with obstacles

Counselling is not an easy road to travel; neither is self-counselling. The title of this book could have been *Self-Counselling Made Easy*, but that might have misled you into thinking that the process *is* easy. The journey of self-awareness is not easy, but it is rewarding. You will come up against obstacles at which you balk. For a time you may feel like giving up; that it is all too hard. You could, like the Israelites, sit by the rivers of your particular Babylon and hang up your harp and refuse to sing. You can wallow in your despair, and sit and complain how hard the journey is. Or you can pick yourself up and look for a way around, over or under the obstacle. Later we shall discuss the use of imagery to help you on your journey, but here is an exercise as a taster.

EXERCISE 1.1

Using imagery to help you on your way

Sit quietly for a few minutes, and when you are relaxed, move on to the next stage.

1. Imagine you are travelling along a narrow pathway, and find the way blocked by a landslide.

2. It is vital that you continue your journey. Imagine how you would overcome the obstacle.

Turn to the Appendix for a suggested answer.

Journeying towards self-discovery

Being your own counsellor will take you out of your accepted way of thinking about things. Some people might criticise this as being 'pie in the sky' or just fantasy. It might be fantasy, it might be fantastic, but so is the journey towards self-discovery, for it is a journey that has no map, no signposts, no known way, yet countless thousands have travelled this way; and every journey is different. Every pilgrim creates his or her own map and signposts, and every pilgrim finds his or her own solutions to problems. Like Christian in Bunyan's *Pilgrim's Progress*, they are all making their way to some Celestial City, yet for each it is different. Life is a paradox; so is the journey towards self-awareness.

   In this pilgrimage, we may be accompanied by someone like a

counsellor, but we cannot rely on him or her to lead us. And we can only go as far, or as quickly, as we, ourselves, are able and willing. Self-counselling is a bit like learning by correspondence - you go at your own pace. Some students are really focused on the course, and apply themselves to every lesson and the accompanying assignments. Others look upon the lessons as a chore, and the assignments as drudgery. But what they have in common is that they are doing things at their own pace, not being pushed by a zealous (or over-zealous) teacher. So in self-counselling.

IDENTIFYING THE LIMITATIONS OF SELF-COUNSELLING

The question must be asked – should people be their own counsellors? An analogy can be drawn: many people are keen 'amateur' gardeners, and produce wonderful shows of fruit and vegetables. Who would ever dream of suggesting they should only garden if they have a degree in horticulture? What about the DIY person, who can build anything from a wall to a whole house, and then build all the fixtures? The examples are endless. The idea that they should not do it is laughable. Is it any more ridiculous then to suggest that a person should learn to be his or her own counsellor?

But what are the limitations? It would be tempting to state there were none, but that would be untrue. However, it is equally possible that the limitations that apply to any counselling also apply to self-counselling. Counselling is often inappropriate for the more florid mental illnesses, but even here, a degree of self-counselling might help; it certainly would be unlikely to make the condition worse.

A second possible reason why self-counselling might not be feasible is the degree to which the person is enmeshed in the problem - in other words, how deeply embedded in the unconscious it is. It could be argued that such cases are not suitable for counselling, but rather for psychoanalysis.

Self-counselling might turn a person into an introspective, self-centred egoist. That is true, it might, and so might becoming engaged in counselling. Yet, if the self-counsellor listens, really listens, to his or her psyche, that inner voice will guide them. However, it is still the self-counsellor's right to become egocentric, and it should not be denied them. Maybe the person needs to become egocentric and self-interested in order to reach a part that hitherto has been inaccessible.

Seeking outside help

The self-counsellor could become enmeshed in feelings that are too difficult to handle. On such occasions the client might feel that the very foundations are being shaken. The self-counsellor might need to withdraw for a time, to regain some stability, or seek the help of an experienced counsellor.

This is linked to another limitation - self-protection. In counselling, where the counsellor interprets what is going on, the client might be presented with interpretations for which he or she is not yet ready. In self-counselling it is very unlikely that the person will reach interpretations or self-observations before being ready to receive them.

A corollary of this is that even if the psyche presents the self-counsellor with what seems an unpalatable 'truth' or insight, the knowledge that it comes from 'within' and was not arrived at by someone else, working to a particular frame of reference or theory, will give the self-counsellor confidence to at least examine it closely and not reject it out of hand, because it is too painful. Also, if the self-counsellor's psyche does present a certain truth, then it could be assumed that the person will have the strength to receive it. The role of the psyche is to work with us towards wholeness.

Self-counselling demands courage, self-sacrifice, initiative and perseverance. Unlike face-to-face counselling, the self-counsellor travels the road, climbs the mountain, swims the ocean, alone, accompanied only by the ever-present psyche.

CASE STUDY

James changes direction
Note:
> James will feature throughout the book. His case study will point to various principles and processes.

James, a man of 30, came into psychiatric nursing, having spent the ten previous years as an advertising salesman. The job had become increasingly irritating to him. He felt his life lacked real motive and satisfaction. Part of the conflict lay in the difference between the demands of the job and his personality. As a salesman he needed to be outgoing, yet he often felt drained and lacking in energy, as if other people were drawing energy from him. As we discussed this, it became clear that he was balanced between being extroverted and introverted.

His new career drew him into a different sort of relationship with others and with himself. He discovered that he was more introspective than he realised, and when I suggested to him that he could profitably spend time on self-counselling (having had six sessions with me), he said he would give it a try, although he was doubtful of how beneficial it would be. He borrowed Horney's *Self-Analysis* and after reading through it, he was convinced that this was something he could do.

SUMMARY

Self-counselling, like self-analysis, is an option for people who are interested in self-development. If in the process you feel a loss of equilibrium which creates anxiety, then think about seeking help from a counsellor before continuing with your self-counselling.

Embarking on self-counselling places you very firmly in the driving seat, with your psyche as your companion alongside you. For self-counselling to be effective, you have to work in partnership with your psyche, in much the same way that counsellor and client work together in a co-operative partnership. When insights come, they blossom straight from your inner self, unadulterated by someone else's thoughts and feelings. They are meant for you, just at this moment.

Being your own counsellor means learning to trust that part of yourself that you cannot see; that part of you that functions to enhance your well-being. Being your own counsellor will increase your self-confidence, for you will have demonstrated that you have the courage to go where you have never gone before.

Self-counselling, as one of the processes of self-awareness, need never end. There will always be fresh insights to work towards; new parts that need to be examined; thoughts, feelings and behaviours to put under the microscope. If the process makes you a more transparent person, with more understanding of yourself and other people, then the process is working. As Karen Horney says, 'Life is struggle and striving, development and growth, and analysis (self-counselling) is one of the means that can help in this process.'

2
Defining the Principles of Self-Counselling

Self-counselling is an aid to self-development. It can act as a spring-board to exploring many avenues which lead to greater understanding of self and of other people. This latter point should not be glossed over; if self-understanding does not also lead to greater understanding of others, then it is a sterile exercise.

If our aim is to reduce the way we blame other people for what happens to us, then the only way we will ever know that it has worked is by change in our behaviour. If our aim is to have more self-confidence, then if we don't act self-confidently, neither we nor anyone else will know that our self-counselling has worked.

All this means is that what we take in must be given out in some way. We may have all the self-knowledge in the world, but unless we show that awareness to others by understanding them, we are, as so succinctly put by St Paul, 'as sounding brass or a tinkling cymbal'.

If our self-counselling does not make us more tolerant, more empathic, less judgmental, then what have we achieved? If we can notch up one change, however small, then we have achieved something significant. If we have gained some insight into what motivates us to behave the way we do, even though changing that behaviour may take the rest of our lives to work out, then we have achieved a great deal.

IDENTIFYING THE ROLE OF THE PSYCHE AS INNER GUIDE

Several times I have referred to the 'psyche'. The oldest, and most general view of the 'psyche' is that held by the early Greeks, who regarded it as 'soul', or the very essence of life. The term derives from classical mythology, and the heroine in the story of Cupid and Psyche. In Greek folklore the soul was pictured as a butterfly – another meaning of both 'psyche' and 'soul'.

The four main functions of the psyche, according to analytical (Jungian) psychology, are Intuition, Sensing, Thinking and Feeling. Each approaches reality from a different point of view and with a different question, and grasps a different part of reality.

One of the fundamental tenets of analytical psychology is that whenever circumstances of life, traumas, deaths, frightening dreams, problems that seem insoluble, attempt to throw us off balance, the psyche constantly strives to maintain inner equilibrium; a bit like an internal gyroscope.

The psyche knows no limitations; it is all-knowing; it knows us intimately, like a glove knows the hand it encloses. The psyche does not have to get to know us; it is us. The psyche does not work from without in, but bathes us in its own light, so that dark spots are transformed from within out. It is as if the psyche is a bright spotlight shining on the stage as we perform the dance of life. As we move so does the spotlight. We cannot escape its searching power. It goes on revealing to us (if we are open to its message) what we need to change in order to continue travelling along the road towards self-awareness and wholeness.

EXERCISE 2.1

Getting in touch with your psyche

Take a few minutes to get comfortable and relaxed. You might find that it helps to close your eyes, but this is not essential.

1.   Imagine you are travelling through a pitch-black tunnel. How do you feel?

2.   Above you a powerful spotlight is switched on. It shines right into you, and shows up the things you need to change.

3.   Watch as the light moves from one thing to another. How do you feel?

4.   The light travels with you, and you reach the end of the tunnel and move into the daylight.

5.   Spend time making a list of all the things the light revealed to you.

Choose one as the focus for your future work on self-counselling. Create a short statement that expresses your feelings about what has happened, and how you would like to change.

TAKING RESPONSIBILITY

Self-counselling places responsibility where it clearly belongs – with you. You cannot hide behind the excuse that the counsellor did not understand you; that you weren't listened to; that the going was too hard. The psyche will laugh at such excuses. The psyche will recognise (much more clearly than any counsellor) when you have reached the limit, or that you are not quite ready to challenge yourself, or that you are not yet ready (or willing) to trade something for something better. The psyche encourages the highest sense of self-responsibility.

Remember: the psyche is not a separate part of us. It is the entire self- body, mind and spirit. Yet it goes beyond and above this trinity, and enters the realm of the spiritual. In this context, spiritual does not mean 'religious'; that is too narrow an interpretation.

While the psyche is not a separate entity, it is helpful to visualise it in some concrete form – as the spotlight, for example. You may find another image suits you better. You may give it human form, with a name, so that you can hold a conversation with it. Try not to be put off by what might seem bizarre; in imagination, anything is permissible, and anything can happen!

LEARNING TO USE FREE ASSOCIATION

Free association is a psychoanalytical technique which taps into the unconscious mind. Three assumptions operate:

- that all lines of thought tend to lead to what is significant

- that your unconscious will lead the associations towards what is significant

- that resistance is minimised by relaxation, but concentration increases it.

The basic rule of free association is that you take note of everything that comes into your mind, without any attempt to control or bring reason to bear. 'Everything' means thoughts, feelings, ideas, even if they are dis- agreeable, even if they seem unimportant or nonsensical. 'Everything' may include views and opinions, past experiences, flashes of fantasy, religion, morals, the quarrel with someone, ambitions; the list is endless, yet everything has a place, and a specific meaning for you. If your psy- che is leading you, then ask, 'why has this come up now? What is the meaning?'

Example of part of a free association period
I sit in my comfortable armchair, take several deep breaths, and start

relaxing my body. At some time during my period of free association I think of a tree, and the association goes something Like this: *tree, oak, Navy, hammock, submarine, Woodlands, sadness.* I start to feel tearful. From my experience I know that I should not analyse each bit of the association, but wait until it is finished. My tears bring me back to the present, and I start the analysis.

Tree. I move from the general to the specific, the specific being what something means to me. In a general sense, the tree represents stability and permanence. It could represent my family tree. But as I dwell on its meaning, I realise it is speaking to me of strength, of being well-rooted and also being productive.

To the specific. It could be any tree, but the next word is *oak*. 'Hearts of oak', a naval march. I served in the *Navy* just after the war, working mainly in a mental hospital. Some happy memories, some not so happy, yet a time of tremendous psychological growth.

Hammock: one of my 'gifts' from the Navy was a hammock, in which I slept for 18 months of my two years, then took it home with me when I was released.

I had the opportunity of applying to be the 'medic' on a *submarine*, but even as I think of that I shudder, for I have never been able to feel comfortable in enclosed spaces. Thought – where does that come from? I allow my mind to wander, and I see myself at about the age of ten, in a grain tank, feeling terrified that I couldn't touch the bottom. I allow the terror of that experience to wash over me. Then I recalled being dared to crawl through a drainpipe; again I feel the terror, recalling how I imagined the pipe rolling down the hill and me trapped inside. These are new feelings.

Woodlands. This was my parents' farm, bought just before I was released from the Navy. Happy days. Marriage, children. Why *sadness*? My part of the business failed, and we were forced to sell all our lovely animals. Is that all? No. Woodlands is no more; it was burned down after my parents retired. Is that all? No. Both parents are now dead, and I still miss them. The tears prick my eyes.

IDENTIFYING DIFFICULTIES IN FREE ASSOCIATION

It is possible that free association is not for everyone. Some people take to it like the proverbial duck to water; others shy away from anything approaching introspection. Free association is not a miracle-worker, neither is it a panacea. But if it is persevered with, and undertaken with as much dedication as learning any other skill, the majority of people will find it answers many of their questions, and certainly shows the inner workings of the mind.

The following types of people might experience difficulty working with free association, but that does not mean that they should not try:

- people who steer clear of anything to do with self-development

- people who have difficulty with intimate relationships

- people who cannot make judgements for themselves; who are afraid to speak lest what they say does not meet with approval

- people who are so caught up in the trap of their conflicts that their whole life is over-controlled by negative thinking

- people who would be so ashamed by what free association reveals that they would feel safer if they never started.

EXERCISE 2.2

Starting to use free association

Spend time getting yourself comfortable and relaxed. Imagine you are looking at a cinema screen, upon which a picture will be projected. If you find this difficult, just let your mind wander, until a word, a thought, a feeling comes to you. Another suggestion is that you imagine you are drifting down a stream on a raft. As you pass, you see certain people, places, incidents that have meaning for you. Do not stop and dwell on any one thing, but, as in the example given above, let your mind make associations. You may do this for five minutes or longer. Your psyche will tell you when it is time to end. Trust it!

Do not make notes while you are free associating, for that would interrupt the stream of consciousness. When you feel the association has ended, then you start making notes, but don't break the recall by analysing them. You may wonder if you will be able to recall all the material. You may consider yourself to have a not very good memory; you might not, but your psyche has the perfect memory. Trust it!

Start with the last word, idea or feeling, and work back to the beginning, jotting down just words or short phrases. Don't fret if you cannot remember every single one. You might recall the missing ones at the next stage. One of the things about memory is that it improves with use. The more you practise accurate recall, the easier it will become.

When you have completed your list (and I suggest that you keep a special notebook for your free associations), then you can start making connections, and exploring themes. What you will probably discover is that not everything comes at once. When you are psychologically ready, and not before, the psyche will reveal more. From time to time read what you have written, and take heart at the progress you have made since you started. Another way is to have a tape recorder running while you are free associating. You might feel a bit strange talking aloud, but if you are used to talking to yourself, that should not present too much of a problem.

In the Appendix (page 120) you will find a list of themes which you can use as triggers for your free association.

CASE STUDY

James faces the truth

One of the areas James and I discussed was that he was (in his words) too fond of judging people. This involved him in telling them what he thought they should be doing, and not doing. He felt that his own moral standards were 'right', and that the world would be a better place if people behaved like him.

In order for James to practise free association he had to make an agreement with his wife, Jenny, so that at a specific time, when the bedroom door was closed, no interruptions, short of a major disaster, would be allowed. He liked the idea of using a tape recorder. He tried to set a regular time weekly, so far as his shifts would allow.

In one of his sessions he achieved what for him was a monumental insight. He had been thinking (and talking) about his ward assessment, where a senior nurse commented on his attitude of 'always blaming other people'. This had led to an argument, then later to James apologising, and promising to look at his attitude.

In his next free association session he started with the word 'blame', and the final theme was just one word, 'victim'. In between the start and finish James recalled many instances to which the word blame was attached. As he meditated on the victim theme, he recalled his feelings of being a victim at the hands of an abusive teacher at his Junior school. His father told him to 'be a man'. James felt helpless. He now realised that he judged other people to put himself in the right; and that he blamed other people to divert attention from himself. He was able to share his insights with me, and then, at a later stage, with the members of his team.

SUMMARY

Critics of self-analysis (and by implication, self-counselling) would argue that it results in a person becoming totally self-engrossed. One way to guard against this is to ensure that change in behaviour accompanies inner changes.

You need the two-way interchange between yourself and other people. If you are achieving insights and skills, then in some way perhaps you can help other people to work towards achieving insights too. By looking outwards as well as inwards, you will achieve a balance that will prevent your becoming self-centred and egotistical.

If at this stage you find the language of 'psyche', 'inner world', and 'travelling companion' uncomfortable, stay with that feeling, and use free association to track the origins of that unease. In that way you will have added another valuable insight.

3
Learning how to Develop
Self-Awareness Insights

Developing a skill without the necessary grasp of the principles would be like an engineer trying to build a house without having the ability to read a blueprint, or being able to understand what was meant by stresses and strains. So far as self-counselling is concerned, the development of insights and self-awareness are crucial, if anything worthwhile is to be achieved.

IDENTIFYING SELF

The self can be thought of as having three regions, as illustrated in Figure 1.

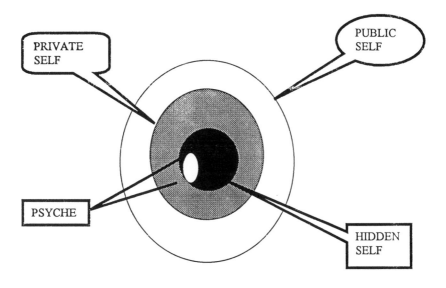

Fig. 1. The three regions of self.

The region of the public self

This is the region that is freely available to ourselves and to other people. It is as if we have little to hide. It is what Charles H Cooley referred to as the *looking-glass effect*, based on how we think other people see and evaluate us (which, of course, is not necessarily how they *do* see us).

The region of the private self

The contents of this part we keep private, or at best reveal only to a limited circle of people whom we trust. Within this region we are aware that we possess an *actual* self and an *ideal* self. The ideal self is what we know we could be, should be, or would like to be. (See *Building Self-Esteem: How to Replace Self-Doubt with Confidence and Well-Being*, William Stewart, How To Books, 1998.) The material in this region is not so accessible as it is in the public region, but more accessible than that which is in the hidden region.

The region of the hidden self

This is the region of which we are but dimly aware – in Jungian terms, the region of the Shadow. The Shadow is the thing we have no wish to be; the negative, dark, primitive side of ourselves; that which is inferior, worthless, uncontrollable and unacceptable.

In psychoanalytic language this is the region of the unconscious, seething with repressed desires, thoughts, feelings and wishes, which influence our current thoughts, feelings and behaviour. Freud proposed that when thoughts, feelings, wishes and desires are unacceptable, they are repressed into the unconscious – out of sight out of mind, as it were. The theory is that all this repression takes place at an early age, and that all neuroses stem from such repression. The task of psychoanalysis is to bring into the conscious that which has been repressed.

Another view is that feelings, thoughts and events are forgotten, overlaid by the more recent. Possibly the answer lies in a mixture of both. Certain feelings, thoughts and events of early childhood do take place before conscious memory. Equally, events that take place within memory may be forgotten, but still influence feelings in the now, as I demonstrated in the example I gave of being trapped in a grain tank. How it affects me now is that I feel very odd when watching people crawling through narrow spaces.

Exploring the role of the psyche

The psyche accesses all three regions, spotlighting the darkest parts. This is what happens in self-counselling, as the psyche lights up what it knows you can handle, yet leaving other parts untouched until you are ready to handle them.

EXERCISE 3.1

Identifying parts of your self

1. Thinking of Cooley's idea of the looking-glass self, how far do you portray yourself as you wish others to see you, rather than be your true self?

2. How far is your self-concept governed by social expectations?

3. Taking the concepts of the 'actual' and 'ideal' self, how close are these two 'selves', or how far apart are they?

4. How much time during the past week have you devoted to your own self-development?

5. In what areas are there discrepancies between your private and public selves? Are you a different person with different people, and who are they?

The basic components of self are listed in Figure 2.

---

1. I am one person.

2. I am the same person now as I was yesterday and as I will be tomorrow.

3. I can distinguish between myself and the rest of the world as being not me.

4. I know that I am thinking, feeling and doing.

5. I have an accurate mental perception of my body.

6. I have positive standards, ideals and ambitions which form my conscious goals.

Fig. 2. The basic components of self.

EXPLORING WHAT SELF-AWARENESS MEANS

Self-awareness is being aware of our physical, mental, emotional, moral, spiritual and social qualities which, together, make us unique individuals; they are all working together to help us towards our fullest potential.

Self-counselling hinges on our ability to explore our own inner world. It is doubtful if any of us truly *knows* who we are. Life is a constant discovery about parts of us that have, until that moment, remained hidden from our conscious knowledge. Indeed many of us would rather be thought of by others in a way other than our true self. Yet this, by itself, can put us under great pressure. Generally it is less stressful to be true than to be false.

There is no guarantee that being self-aware will bring 'happiness' – a very transient feeling – however, it will bring a certain sense of wholeness. You can never say, 'I have arrived.' But you can say, 'I am arriving.'

Kahil Gibran, in *The Prophet*, says this about self knowledge:

> But let there be no scales to weigh your unknown treasures;
> And seek not the depths of your knowledge with staff or sounding line.
> For self is a sea boundless and measureless.
> Say not, 'I have found the truth,' but rather, 'I have found a truth.'
> Say not, 'I have found the path of the soul,'
> Say rather, 'I have met the soul walking upon my path.'
> For the soul walks upon all paths.
> The soul walks not upon a line, neither does it grow like a reed.
> The soul unfolds itself, like a lotus of countless petals.

Self-knowledge is a quest, and an essential part of self-counselling. Self-knowledge will enhance your self-counselling; self-counselling will, in return, enhance your self-knowledge. Self-knowledge is to self-counselling as the glove is to the hand.

EXERCISE 3.2

Using your Life Chart to develop your self-awareness

This section is based on the work of Adolf Meyer (1866-1950), an influential Swiss-American psychiatrist, much of whose teaching has been incorporated into psychiatric theory and practice. His work appears in his *Collected Papers* (four volumes, 1950-2) and *Psychobiology* (1957).

This exercise will take some time, and you may find it easier to spread it over several sessions.

1. Start from your birth date, and using the Chart in the Appendix (page 122), plot your life up to the present. You might not remember your birth! But what were the circumstances surrounding that momentous event? Were you a 'wanted' child? Where do you come in the family?

2. Record anything significant, such as illness, presents, changes in the family, school, college or university, first boyfriend/girlfriend, marriage, children, and so on.

3. Pay particular attention to recalling your thoughts, feelings and behaviours associated with the events. This can be considered in two strands: as you were at the time, and as you now feel about them.

4. Use the Chart as a basis for deeper exploration of your past life. You may find it helpful to talk to your family about specific happenings. They might be able to fill in some of the details.

As you progress through life, you can use this Chart to add to your self-awareness. As you explore the various stages of your life, don't rush over them; use free association to plumb the depths of what hitherto might only have been vague memories. Be cautious about with whom you share the intimate details of your Life Chart!

USING MASLOW'S HIERARCHY OF HUMAN NEEDS TO ENHANCE YOUR SELF-AWARENESS

Abraham H Maslow (1908-70), a US psychologist and philosopher best known for his self-actualisation theory of psychology, proposed that the primary goal of psychotherapy should be the integration of the self. Maslow argued that each person has a hierarchy of needs that must be satisfied (see Figure 3).

The theory is that only as each need is satisfied are we motivated to reach for the next higher level; thus, people who lack food or shelter or who cannot feel themselves to be in a safe environment are unable to concentrate on higher needs.

Our drive for self-actualisation may conflict with our rights and duties and responsibilities to other people who are involved.

While I might be high on self-actualisation today, tomorrow something could happen that would change that, and thrust me back into satisfying the basic needs. For example, if I were made redundant from my job then however much I might want to continue the upward climb

Self-actualisation – The level of personal growth, which may be met through the challenge of creativity, or demanding greater achievement. Self-actualising behaviours include risk-taking, seeking autonomy and freedom to act.

Ego-status – Related to status within a group, ambition and a desire to excel.

Belongingness – The need for relationships to be appreciated and accepted: met through family ties and membership of groups.

Safety – Security, orderliness, protective rules, and risk avoidance: met by salary, insurance policies, alarm systems.

Basic – Physiological and survival needs: met by food, shelter, clothing, sex.

Fig. 3. Maslow's hierarchy of needs, pictured as a ladder.

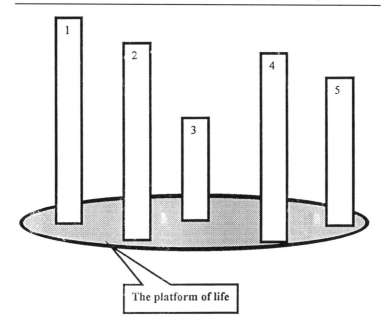

Key:

1 = Basic needs   2 = Survival needs   3 = Belongingness
4 = Ego-status   5 = Self-actualisation

Fig. 4. Maslow's five basic needs.

towards reaching my potential, my prime concern is likely to be trying to find another job trying to meet the security needs. If I were flying over the desert and the plane crashed, my immediate need would be very basic, food and water, not self-actualisation.

Another way of looking at Maslow's model is that rather than moving on from stage to stage, as in climbing a ladder, all five needs are being met simultaneously, to some degree, as in Figure 4.

EXERCISE 3.3

Identifying your needs

Imagine each of the five columns in Figure 4 are five identical tanks, and you are filling them to represent where you see yourself now.

1.   What would be the level of each tank?

2.   How do you reckon you fulfil each of the five needs?

3.   How much do other people help you fulfil those needs?

4.   How much do you think you help other people fulfil their needs?

5.   What have you done recently to fulfil your ego-status needs?

6.   What have you done recently to fulfil your self-actualisation needs?

7.   Look back over the past year and see what personal growth you have achieved.

CASE STUDY

James reconstructs his Life Chart (the first eight years)

James had one advantage over some people, he kept a diary, and had done so for years. Thus it was relatively simple for him to reconstruct his Life Chart. He said to me, 'This is going to be easy. It's all there.' But although the details were there, at least from the age of eight, filling in the gaps before that age, and then tapping into the feelings, proved far from easy.

Writing of his birth, he said, 'I was a replacement child, my parents having lost a child, run over at the age of five. Thinking about my birth I feel privileged, but also a weight of responsibility. Although I never knew John, I feel that I miss him.' He then went on to say how even thinking about his dead brother filled him with longing, as if a part of him was missing. This led him to make links with the way he related to people. He needed other people, but he was always afraid they would be taken from him.

The next significant event was his mother being taken ill when James was about four years old. He recalled his father being anxious, and very short-tempered, nothing unusual. He recalled the ambulance taking her away, and the feeling of emptiness in the house. 'Mum was the one who kept the home going.' He wrote, 'As I'm writing this now, I feel tearful. Am I tapping into the feelings I had then?' Then he wrote of the joy when mother came out of hospital. Then he had a flash of insight. 'Is that why I'm terrified if Jenny complains of not feeling well? Am I afraid of losing her?' He went on to relate that with the birth of each of their two children he hadn't felt afraid, 'For that wasn't an illness.'

James liked school. Disciplined for stealing a penny from one of the other pupils. Sent to the headteacher. Feelings of disgrace and guilt. He wrote, 'Is this tied up with my wanting to blame other people, and always needing to judge them?'

The next incident was when James himself was taken to hospital with meningitis. He spoke of 'a bleak time, painful memories - physical and emotional. Had a near-death experience. Felt an obligation to serve God. This created great conflict between good and evil within me.' He wrote, 'That's the first time I've ever said that, even to myself. Good and evil. Two sides of the coin? Two parts of me? I'll have to work on that!'

SUMMARY

Being self-aware does not mean we are as transparent as the purest glass. Being aware of self means just that; striving to know who we are, our faults and failings, our good points and strengths. It also does not mean that we have nothing to hide from other people; it means that we are selective about what we reveal and to whom. It does not mean that we have worked through all our problems and difficulties; it does mean that we still have foibles and quirks, but that we are seeking to understand them and how they influence our lives and our behaviour.

Becoming aware of self means that we are prepared to dip into the regions of our personal underworld. It may mean that we have to fight with fearsome feelings and memories which influence our lives. But it may also mean us getting in touch with what is beautiful and worthy. For rarely is our quest solely concerned with discovering the dark. One of the functions of the psyche is to help us transform the bad and the ugly into the good and beautiful.

4
Learning how to Work with your Dreams

Analysis of dreams provides valuable information about our unconscious inner conflicts. Dreams more often arise from the hidden self, and all have a message; the task is to find that message. The task is not made easier by the fact that dreams are couched in symbolic terms. Yet they direct our attention to what we are in most danger of not seeing, or neglecting.

Dreams can work for us. Most of us know how we have gone to sleep with a problem on our mind. When we wake next day, the answer 'comes'. One night in 1865 Friedrich August Kekule, having been thwarted in finding the final bit of a puzzle, dreamt of a snake biting its tail (the Ouroboros). From that dream his concept of the six-carbon benzene ring was born.

Some dreams are transparent; these probably arise from the public region of the self. Others come like encrypted messages on the Internet, for which we need a decoder. Free association can help to decode the hidden message.

An understanding of symbols and symbolic language will help your understanding of your dreams. There are various books on the use of symbols listed in the Further Reading section at the end of this book.

EXERCISE 4.1

Enlisting the aid of your psyche
The psyche has access to all three regions of the self, but unlike us, the psyche never sleeps; in fact it is at its most active when the control we exercise over ourselves is relaxed in sleep.

1. Get yourself comfortable, and recall a recent dream.

2. Don't analyse it, but let as much of it replay as it will.

3. Now imagine the spotlight of the psyche shining upon your dream.

4. Hitherto hidden bits of the dream will be revealed, and you will begin to understand some of the meanings.

5. Don't rush the process. As the spotlight moves around your dream, take note of all that is highlighted – shapes, colours, people, actions, places, feelings and thoughts.

6. When you have explored the dream enough, gently 'come to' and then make notes of what you have experienced.

Dreams often reflect our inner conflicts. By taking note of our dreams we can work with the psyche towards greater understanding. Dreams, if we give them credit, and seek to understand them, are incredibly honest. If we are not prepared to heed the dream messages, they will stop coming.

TWO DIFFERENT APPROACHES TO DREAM INTERPRETATION

Perhaps the most famous and highly systematised approach to interpreting and using dreams in therapy is that developed by Sigmund Freud in *The Interpretation of Dreams* (1900, translated by James Strachey and reprinted in Penguin Books, 1991). His analysis of his own dreams – an essential part of this self-analysis – is reckoned to be the most revealing psychological introspection ever recorded. Freud referred to dreams as 'the royal road to the unconscious'.

In Freud's view, the task of a dream is to bring unconscious desires to consciousness, disguised in symbolic images; these are ordinarily kept out of consciousness (repressed), because they represent forbidden impulses, often of a sexual nature.

Jung's theories are different from those of Freud. For Jung, dreams are forward-looking, creative, instructive and, to some extent, prophetic. Jung believed that dreams draw on the collective unconscious. Archetypes are the common symbols, which enshrine universal, even mystical perceptions and images. Dreams serve to enlarge our insight into our own resources, and contain hints on how to solve our own problems.

RECORDING YOUR DREAMS

Try to avoid waking up too quickly, even though you are anxious to record the dream. Record the dream as you recall it. The sequence, if it is important, can come later. Don't be tempted to think (I speak from experience!) 'Oh, I'll remember that in the morning.' The odds are against you! If you wake from a dream, your psyche is telling you to record it.

Don't be shy about what you record. At the same time, be circumspect about who has access to it. Unless you can be certain that what you record will be as safe as Fort Knox, then your psyche will not feel free to operate, and your dreams will have little meaning. You may, however, be incredibly open and not mind if others do read.

If you are artistic, you might like to draw or paint parts of your dreams.

When the dream is fully recorded, spend time in a relaxed state and let your psyche take you back over the dream. If you expect insights and revelations, you will get them, although they may not always be what you want, or come in the way you expect. Dream work, as in all self-counselling, demands absolute honesty with yourself. There is no point in trying to deceive your psyche.

INTERPRETING YOUR DREAMS

Using dictionaries

Get yourself two good dictionaries: one of symbols and another of dreams. Remember, a dictionary is only a general guide. You must search for the meaning specific to you. Be wary of the interpretations that come ready-made in dream books. However, the more you read, the more understanding you will have. Above all, what you dream is your dream, and while there may be certain similarities with the dream of your twin, if you have one, it is still unique to you, because it comes from your own self, brought to light by your own psyche.

Exploring the details

Study the atmosphere of the dream – the emotional content. Was it predominantly fearful, joyful, sexual, spiritual? Was there terror, violence, speed, falling, travelling through space? Did you feel abandoned, weepy, affectionate, jealous, sad?

- What was the precise dream content?
- What was the weather doing?
- How were people dressed?
- What colours did you see?
- Were there any animals, and were they friendly or hostile?

Note: In dreams, 'people' might not refer to gender, but to the qualities of male or female. Similarly, a kitten in a dream might represent a playful child, possibly you.

- What was the precise location? For example, a dream of a graveyard would have a different meaning from witnessing a wedding.

- What was the reason for a particular symbol, in that specific spot? Was it natural, or was it out of place, or incongruous? For example, a tree appearing in the middle of a lake has a different meaning from a tree on a lawn.

- What was your overall feeling as you awakened? Try to discover any psychological conflicts. Take special note of any recurrent dreams or themes. What is your psyche drawing to your attention? What have you not yet resolved?

- Take note of what appear to be puns, and jokes, especially those that have you laughing. Dream analysis is not always deadly serious; it has its amusing side, too.

Looking for connections

Look for links or themes between various dreams. This means going over your previous dreams, maybe several times. Use free association, especially when the interpretation eludes you. Try not to think that you have to get an instant answer, like instant coffee. Sometimes the psyche will bring to light a fragment of something from the past, a bit of jigsaw, and leave the rest to you to get at through free association.

Becoming the characters or objects in your dreams

One useful way of getting at the meaning of dreams is to become the various parts of the dream. If you saw a bird flying overhead, become the bird.

- What does it see?
- Where is it going?
- Where has it come from?

Speak to the bird. Ask it what message it has for you. If you stumbled over a rock, become the rock. What is it in your life that is causing you to stumble? A stumbling block. Who put it there? How long has it been there? How can you change it into a stepping stone? Try not to be constrained by 'logical' or linear thinking. Try to develop the habit of lateral or creative thinking. This theme will be discussed in detail in Chapter 5.

Gaining a general impression

If a dream is long and complicated, try to get a general impression. What was the overall message/theme/purpose? What was the beginning, middle, end?

EXERCISE 4.2

Interpreting your own dream

Take a dream you have recently had. Using the following outline, try to interpret your dream.

- Antecedents – what actual circumstances led up to the dream.

- Atmosphere.

- Feelings, expressed.

- Feelings, implied.

- People.

- Symbols.

- Conflicts.

- Links with previous dreams.

LEARNING TO RECOGNISE RESISTANCE

Self-counselling through dreams is not without its difficulties. One of these is resistance. In psychoanalysis, resistance is the patient's unconscious efforts to thwart the aims and process of therapy. The patient does this by blocking unconscious, repressed material from breaking through into the conscious.

In dreams, the resistance is similar; you are afraid that you won't be able to handle what will be revealed – part of that Shadow; the undesired self.

- You may become aware of resistance by a feeling of being blocked, or of frustration that the 'answer' won't come, or that when you engage in free association, you keep going round in circles, seemingly getting nowhere.

- You may suffer from a punitive conscience which (unconsciously) tells you that it is unsafe to know too much about yourself. Linked to this is that part of you may be telling you that you lack the skill to be your own counsellor, and that it is all wasted effort.

- You may be refusing to co-operate with your psyche. This involves arguing against what is revealed, not exploring possibilities, but rejecting them out of hand. Often this is associated with 'That is silly.'

- Resistance may also show itself as always wanting to accept the generalisation of, for example, a symbol, and not probe beneath the surface to find the meaning specific to you. You may not want to 'feel' the feelings that dreams generate. You may intellectualise what is happening and trivialise them.

- You may fail to keep to the contract you have with yourself. For example, you may 'forget' to record your dreams, making excuses that you are too tired, late for work, and so on.

LEARNING TO DEAL WITH RESISTANCE

The conscious mind strives to maintain the status quo. It does not like change. Working with dreams challenges the established position. If you can identify at least one facet of resistance, you are part-way to dealing with it.

Let the psyche show you how to get through the barrier. It may mean that you have to go back a stage or two, and deal with some unfinished business before you can move forward. If you feel like giving up 'all this nonsense', then is the time to ask your psyche for help. You could be on the verge of a breakthrough.

Using free association, and the word 'resistance' as a trigger, spend time tracking where the resistance comes from. You might discover that it lies in a previous insight, which, if you continue making that link, will move you forward and upward.

If your resistance is a reaction to genuine tiredness, then you must take steps to remedy the situation. Going round in circles might indicate resistance, or it might mean that there is unfinished business to attend to. Either way, ask your psyche to shed light. Use the word 'circle' in free association, and discover where it leads you.

Above all, be patient with yourself. Be kind to yourself. Everest wasn't scaled in a day. Your mountain is just as high. Resistance cannot be crushed; it can only be worked through.

CASE STUDY

James dreams about boats

James was well on his way with free association when he came to me with a dream. James had been working on the relationship with his father. 'He's not a man to talk to. I often wish we could have a proper conversation, but he can't, or won't.' The earlier relationship had been quite physical, sometimes ending up in fights.

He related this dream. 'I was on a boat, on a sunny day, which clouded over, within the lock in a canal. I couldn't decide which direction I should be travelling in. In the end I decided to go up-stream. If there was anyone at the helm, it wasn't me. I felt frustrated that the lock gate took so long to open. When it eventually did, we moved upstream. Then after a while my father appeared and took over. I felt OK about that. Then he vanished, but I still wasn't sure if I was in charge.'

EXERCISE 4.3

Interpreting James's dream

1. Use the knowledge you have gained so far to identify the various parts of James's dream.

2. What would be your interpretation of this dream?

Turn to the Appendix (page 122) for a suggested answer.

SUMMARY

If Freud is correct, that dreams are the royal road to the unconscious, then studying dreams is a sure way of gaining more insight into our particular underworld. If you look upon dreams as one of the psyche's ways of helping you towards self-awareness, then they will come as heralds of light, not of darkness. Their aim is the development of your personality, not to destroy you.

Taking Jung's stance, dreams are creative, they tap into the collective unconscious, that part which we share with the whole of humankind, past, present and future. Thus you might find it more helpful not to interpret your dreams too rigidly, but to work with the overall feelings. Dreams are seldom rational; thus if the dream is to be fully understood, interpretation should be approached with delicate care. You will know when you hit the right notes, for they will set your spirit tingling with excitement.

Any skill takes time to master. Working with dreams is no different. So, be patient. Perhaps patience is one of the qualities your psyche is urging you to develop.

5
Cultivating your Power of Imagery

USING YOUR IMAGINATION

This chapter is an introduction to the fascinating world of imagination and its use in self-counselling. Imagery taps into the vast wealth of symbols and symbolic language, myths, legends, fairy-tales, folklore, superstitions and allusions. This particular mode of working may present difficulties to some people, who must always look for explanation, who always see things in black or white terms.

The material which emerges during imagery may then be analysed in terms of its meaning and symbolism – similar to dream analysis. Interpretation of symbols must be tentative. There is a literal interpretation which is obvious. A key opens a door; it may represent a sexual symbol, but it may also represent freedom, coming of age, leaving emotional adolescence behind and moving into emotional adulthood.

Unblocking your feelings

What imagery does is to cut through the control of the mind which so often blocks tapping into the feelings. This does *not* mean that you are *out of control*; that would be too frightening to contemplate, and would certainly not be therapeutic. At all times you are totally aware of what is happening, of where your imagination is taking you, although the *why* or the *outcome* is obscured.

Your psyche is in control of the operation, and the psyche, if trusted, will work towards wholeness and integration. It also means an active partnership between you and your psyche. Imagery is not an easy option, it demands as much skill, experience and sensitivity as any other approach.

Finding liberation and enlightenment

I hope that this part of your self-counselling journey will be liberating for you. I hope your journey will not be desert-dry, nor as laborious as climbing a mountain, or as depressing as going down into the deepest cave, but if it is like this, please try to use your imagination to

43

understand what is happening, and seek for ways to change the image into a feeling that is more acceptable to you and more enlightening.

EXERCISE 5.1

Making a start on using imagery

Several times in previous chapters I have invited you to use imagery, so you will have already discovered the close similarity of free association to imagery, particularly if you are the sort of person who 'thinks' in pictures. Some people do not 'see' images, they have an inner awareness of an image. Other people 'see' images very clearly.

Start by getting yourself relaxed, but not so that you fall asleep. Think of a word you would like to explore. For example: blemish, bondage, façade, labyrinth, sanctuary, tornado may be trigger words to get you started (see the list in the Appendix, page 125). Meditate on your chosen word, and travel with your imagination where it takes you.

Don't be alarmed (you might be surprised!) at what, or where, your imagination takes you. If you are confronted by an image that alarms you, remember you always have a guide – your psyche – who will protect you. Whatever confronts you is part of yourself, and the fact that it has appeared in your imagination means that now is the time to work on it.

Just as in a dream, from which you can rouse yourself, so with imagery. Your imagination will take you on a journey towards self-discovery. Along this journey you may be led into fields, woods, up mountains, or into streams, lakes or the sea. You may find yourself in a house which looks vaguely familiar, which you realise is yourself. You may find strange objects, which assume bizarre shapes and psychedelic colours. Creatures of the world may appear, some of them speaking to you. All of these are meant just for you. Seek to understand them.

Everything that appears in imagery has meaning, and, like dreams, they often appear in symbolic form. Part of the excitement and the wonder is interpreting the symbols. Much of what is involved in imagery relates to myth and legend, or to fairy-tales, and it is here we see evidence that supports Jung's theory of the collective unconscious.

CASE STUDY

Susan's imaginary journey up a mountain

Susan was feeling uncertain about herself; her self-confidence was low and she used the word 'flat' as an imagery trigger, and found herself part-way up a mountain, on a plateau, overlooking a beautiful valley, with a river running through it. She had stopped for rest. The top of the mountain was still a long way off. She wanted to press on. Although she was on her own, she didn't want a companion. The top looked bright and inviting. She plodded upward, determined to reach the summit. Talking it over with me, Susan said, 'When, I "came to", and it took a long time to come off that mountain and back into the room, I was totally at peace; a rare state for me. It's a long way, William, but I'll make it.'

EXERCISE 5.2

Interpreting Susan's imaginary journey

From what you have already learned about the symbolism of dreams and imagery, how would you interpret Susan's story? You will find a suggested answer in the Appendix (page 126).

IDENTIFYING THE BENEFITS OF USING IMAGINATION

The question is not, 'Why use imagination,' but rather 'Why not use imagination?' or 'Can we avoid using imagination?' Indeed, I would go as far as to say that we cannot really begin to understand our inner world unless we do use imagination.

A word may trigger an image, and an image, a word; and the more specific the word, the more easily the image will be triggered. Abstract words do not easily trigger images, though this is entirely dependent on the word and your experience.

Our minds cannot tell the difference between real experience and one that is vividly and repeatedly imagined. That is a salutary statement, for it we constantly imagine what is negative, our unconscious mind will absorb that. Conversely, if we imagine what is positive, our mind will absorb that. So, working with imagination in self-counselling can help to reverse negative to positive. I make no apologies for such a statement, for I have seen it work in the lives of too many people to attribute the change to chance.

EXERCISE 5.3

Learning to make your imagination work for you

Create an imaginary scene in which:

1. You predict something and it happens.

2. You create a great work that people praise.

3.   Someone deliberately messes up something of yours and you put it right.

4.   You make a speech and receive a standing ovation.

5.   Your boss asks you to draw up a blueprint for an important project and it is a winner.

6.   You invent something that makes your working life easier.

7.   You create a huge hole in the sky, and then fill it with imaginary objects.

8.   You find a map of Treasure Island, then set out to find the treasure.

9.   You are walking along the street and you come face to face with your double.

10. You come face to face with someone you thought was dead.

While doing any imagery exercises, note when you allow your mind to wander. Gently bring your mind back to the latest association. When the association is finished, think around those times you allowed your mind to wander and try to discover the reason why. By recalling in this disciplined way you are controlling your mind.

> **Let your imagination work *for* you, not *against* you.**

End of session exercise
Each time you engage in exercises involving imagery, finish off with the following routine.

1.   Rapidly sketch over the session in your mind.

2.   Make a few notes of what took place and any insights you have received.

3.   Go round and touch various objects to 'ground' you.

4.   Stand upright, stretch your hands above your head, and as you slowly lower them to your sides, repeat, several times, 'I am . . . Today's date is . . . and I am here (name of the room and place).'

Note: Imagery, as well interpretation of dreams, is better avoided if you are feeling emotionally vulnerable. Dealing with deep feelings might prove too traumatic for you.

UNDERSTANDING RIGHT AND LEFT BRAIN FUNCTIONS

A small boy stopped and spoke to a man hitting a rock, and asked him why he was doing it. Michelangelo looked up and replied, 'Because there's an angel inside who wants to come out.'

Creativity involves conscious thinking and ideas, but also tapping into the subconscious – the angel imprisoned within. Powers of imagination and insight exist in the deepest regions of our minds, often unrecognised, and frequently ignored.

The left and right hemispheres of the brain specialise in different activities. The left, 'logical', systematic hemisphere controls movements on the right side of the body. It is more concerned with 'active doing'. The right, 'intuitive' hemisphere controls movements on the left side of the body, and is more concerned with the whole, not parts.

Identifying left brain specialisation

● *Verbal functions*. Language skills, speech, reading and writing, and spelling. Remembers facts, recalls names and dates.

● *Analytical*. Logical and structured. Evaluates data rationally.

● *Linear*. Processes information systematically and in sequence; one-step-at-a-time thinking.

● *Mathematical*. The number-crunching part of the brain.

Identifying right brain specialisation

● *Non-verbal*. Knowledge is achieved through images.

● *Holistic*. Processes various data simultaneously. Sees the whole, and can make leaps of insight. We recognise faces with the right hemisphere.

● *Spatial*. Keeps us knowing where we are – upright or lying down; above or below. Helps us work out puzzles. Creates inner maps to help us find our way around.

● *Musical*. 'Talent' originates in the right brain; musical education enlists the co-operation of both hemispheres.

● *Metaphoric*. The left hemisphere gets confused with metaphors and paradoxes; the right brain 'sees' them with unexplained insight.

● *Imaginative*. It is as if the right brain is a centre set up specifically to house imagination; it is from there we make up stories, work with dreams, enter into the character of a play.

● *Artistic.* All drawing, painting and related subjects are right brain orientated.

● *Emotional.* The right brain is more in touch with feelings than is the left brain. The left brain will tend to 'intellectualise' feelings.

● *Spiritual.* The ability to engage in worship, prayer, meditation and mysticism.

● *Dreams.* These arise primarily in the right brain, sometimes described as the internal poet.

Assessing left and right brain functions

The perfect solution is a harmonious, co-operative working relationship between the two hemispheres. Most of us do use both, but occupation and preference often push us into using one and relatively neglecting the other. When a person is occupied all the working day on a systematic, data processing job, there is little opportunity for the right hemisphere to get to work. Likewise, for someone such as an artist, the left hemisphere might not be used to its full extent.

There is no merit in being either right or left brain orientated; neither is *better* then the other. But self-counselling, with its emphasis on the inner world, makes more demands on the right hemisphere than on the left. While it is comparatively easy to teach a rational, logical approach (provided the pupil is temperamentally suited), we can only *develop* and *train* the right brain functions.

EXERCISE 5.4

Developing your right brain functions

1. Taking the points listed above, calculate how much of your day is taken up with right or left brain functions.

2. Is your job more left than right brain orientated?

3. Are you aware of any talent that you have not developed, or allowed to wither?

4. Make a contract with yourself – today – that you will spend some part of every day developing your creative self.

CASE STUDY

James uses imagery

James relates this story. 'I was working on the ward and engaged in conversation with a patient I'll call Joe, a man in his late 60s. He was being treated for depression, and he wasn't easy to talk to, and there were long silences between us. I began to feel oppressed, as if a blackness was falling on me. Remembering your guidance, I looked at this blackness, and then, quite suddenly I remembered a movie I'd seen which had a scene of the Black Hole of Calcutta in it. I said to Joe, "This feeling I have is that you're trapped in a black hole." "That's right, lad. I am that. How did you guess that's what I was remembering?" He then went on to tell me about his early days in the mines, where one of his jobs (at the age of 14) was to be stuck down a dark shaft, shovelling dross into buckets on a moving escalator. "I did that for eight hours a day; five and a half days a week. Now when I'm feeling low, my mind is dragged back to that black hole."'

SUMMARY

An exciting development over recent years is the work done on right/left brain creativity.

For so long, many of us have been programmed into left brain thinking – logical and analytical, and the acquisition of knowledge. In the process, our right (creative) hemisphere has been relegated to the fourth division. We need to use both.

In imagery, one moves in and out of the collective unconscious, as images raised from the collective unconscious are brought to the surface, images that are charged with powerful feelings.

Using imagery and the right brain might bring you into contact with dragons as well as angels, but both are parts of you. If at any time during self-counselling you feel deeply disturbed by what is happening, take time out, and if the discomfort continues, you might be advised to seek help from an experienced counsellor.

6
Using Transactional Analysis to Assist Self-Development

Transactional Analysis (TA) was developed by Eric Berne (1910-70). Although it is a system of analysis and therapy, and a model for relating to others, it is an invaluable tool to assist self-development and self-awareness.

TA lays great stress on open and direct communication, including intimacy. It is these two points which are particularly appropriate in this chapter, for self-counselling depends upon our ability to communicate honestly with ourselves, and direct and open communication is an essential element in intimacy. Can you be intimate with yourself? The answer is yes. The more we know about ourselves, the more intimate we become with ourselves. People who dislike themselves cannot enjoy personal intimacy. TA will help you explore the parts of yourself which influence your attitude towards yourself as well as how you relate to other people.

IDENTIFYING THE PARENT, ADULT, CHILD STATES

Berne identified what he called ego states, and called them Parent, Adult and Child, normally abbreviated to P-A-C, and capitalised to distinguish them from parent, adult and child (see Figure 5).

We all carry the PAC ego states within us, and sometimes, particularly when under pressure, we resort to responding from an inappropriate state, inappropriate because it tends to bring out behaviour in other people which often results in conflict. Part of self-awareness is to become aware of which state we are in and why. For example, when we get 'hooked into' our Child or Parent ego state it is as if some unfinished business leaves that particular part of us exposed. In order to be truly alive, we need enough Parent to be firm and caring; enough Adult to be fair and objective; and enough Child to be appropriately happy.

EXERCISE 6.1

Identifying your own ego states
From the descriptions given in Figure 5, assess in what situations and with whom you find yourself becoming:

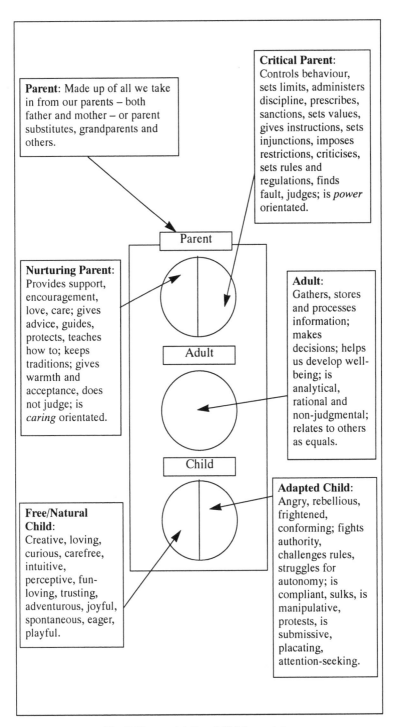

Parent: Made up of all we take in from our parents – both father and mother – or parent substitutes, grandparents and others.

Critical Parent: Controls behaviour, sets limits, administers discipline, prescribes, sanctions, sets values, gives instructions, sets injunctions, imposes restrictions, criticises, sets rules and regulations, finds fault, judges; is *power* orientated.

Nurturing Parent: Provides support, encouragement, love, care; gives advice, guides, protects, teaches how to; keeps traditions; gives warmth and acceptance, does not judge; is *caring* orientated.

Adult: Gathers, stores and processes information; makes decisions; helps us develop well-being; is analytical, rational and non-judgmental; relates to others as equals.

Free/Natural Child: Creative, loving, curious, carefree, intuitive, perceptive, fun-loving, trusting, adventurous, joyful, spontaneous, eager, playful.

Adapted Child: Angry, rebellious, frightened, conforming; fights authority, challenges rules, struggles for autonomy; is compliant, sulks, is manipulative, protests, is submissive, placating, attention-seeking.

Parent

Adult

Child

Fig. 5. Parent, Adult and Child ego states.

- the critical Parent
- the nurturing Parent
- the adapted Child
- the free Child
- the Adult.

Relate the above to behaviour, words, gestures, voice tone. You may find some of these questions soul-searching. But self-awareness would be superficial if it left you feeling comfortable all the time.

UNDERSTANDING THE FOUR LIFE POSITIONS OF TA

Harris, in his book *I'm OK – You're OK*, proposes four emotional positions we can adopt in life. They are:

> I'm not OK, You're not OK.
> I'm not OK, You're OK.
> I'm OK, You're not OK.
> I'm OK, You're OK.

See Figure 6 for a summary of the four life positions of TA.

The developing child (if all goes well) progresses from the first position to the fourth. The amount of recognition, or 'stroking', is what helps the child move towards the final position – I'm OK, You're OK. Moving into the fourth position is a conscious choice, fuelled by a determination to be genuine, and not play games either with other people or with one-self. Games are not pleasure, they are manipulative.

Examples of games people play

1. 'Why don't you?' 'Yes, but.' Person A makes a suggestion. Person B knocks it back. And so it goes on and on until person A gives up the struggle.

2. Wife says to husband, 'If it weren't for you, I would . . .' (the hard-done-by victim). Husband probably responds with, 'You wanted to . . .' (defending the goal area).

3. 'Kick me, I'm no good anyway.' (I'm poor and worthless, and no good. Use me as a doormat.) But when the other person doesn't play the game and refuses to offer sympathy, the first person gets all huffy. 'You don't understand what I'm going through.' (Poor me!)

4. 'If it weren't for you, I would . . .' In this game the person blames everybody else – parents, teachers, society, God – for being what he or she is. Passing the buck would be an apt title for this game.

Life position	Basic attitude	Descriptive words
I'm not OK, You're OK.	My life is not worth much; I'm nothing compared to you. I'm a loser, a victim.	Depression, resignation, suicide.
I'm not OK, You're not OK	Life is not worth anything at all; we might as well be dead. So, it doesn't matter what we do or who we hurt. It's all my fault that nobody loves me.	Futility, alienation, severe withdrawal, despair, rejection.
I'm OK, You're not OK.	I'm going to get what I can though I'm not much. Your life is not worth much; you are dispensable. Get out of my way. I'm top dog. You are inferior.	Arrogant, do-gooder, distrustful, bossy, put-down.
I'm OK, You're OK. (Only this state puts people on equal terms. This is the position of personal autonomy.)	Life is for living; let's live it to the full. We are both winners. I accept myself and you as equals.	Good, healthy, successful, competent, confident, challenging, creative.

Fig. 6. Summary of TA's four life positions.

Giving and receiving 'strokes'

In general, when our Child feels *not OK* we become more used to negative strokes than to positive ones. When we become anxious, threatened or powerless, we have a tendency to slip back into the adapted Child who is frequently rebellious. Which position we choose will depend on our particular childhood experience, and on the quality of the strokes we receive. *Positive* strokes are warm and enhance self-esteem, and evoke the feeling of 'I'm OK, You're OK.' Expressing love, caring, respect, and responding to an expressed need are all positive strokes. *Negative* strokes are cold and knock self-esteem and evoke the feeling of 'I'm not OK'. 'I can't stand you' is a negative stroke.

Victim role
We adopt the role of Victim (without cause) feeling unjustly treated. The Victim colludes with the oppressor, does not admit to feelings of being persecuted, and does not use all of his/her own power to overcome the oppression. If we don't want to be a Victim, we must demand not to be Rescued. We may have to repeat our demand many times, and experience tremendous feelings of guilt about being deprived of the Rescuing role.

Don't play the Drama Game!

Rescuer role
We adopt the role of Rescuer when our helping keeps others dependent on us. True helping is based on the Life Position of 'I'm OK, You're OK.' Rescuing puts the other person in the role of Victim, and implies helplessness and hopelessness, and not being able to manage without our help. We take over, thus relieving the other person of any responsibility for helping him or herself. We do it mainly because rescuing makes us feel good.

Persecutor role
We adopt the Persecutor role when we set unnecessarily strict limits on behaviour or are charged with enforcing the rules, but do so harshly. When we become fed up with being Rescued we generally react against the Rescuer and resist any further attempt to be Rescued, or sabotage the attempt. This eventually turns the rescuer into a Persecutor, and will evoke this sort of response: 'After all I've done for you; all the time I've spent on you; all the money I've given you; look at you, still the same. I wash my hands of you.'

Fig. 7. Identifying the players in the Drama Game.

EXERCISE 6.2

Learning to give strokes

1. Think back to your childhood and try to work out from whom you received the most positive strokes. What were the strokes?

2. What lessons have you learnt from the past? Who do you stroke, and what strokes do you give?

3. What is it that hinders you from giving positive strokes to people?

4. What negative strokes do you give people?

5. Who do you give most negative strokes to?

6. Do you give more positive than negative strokes or vice versa? Remember, we need positive strokes to maintain a sense of well-being. Children who do not receive positive strokes often invite negative strokes, for they are better than no strokes at all.

IDENTIFYING THE RESCUE TRIANGLE

This is one of the games identified by Karpman and is also called the Drama Game. The game is made up of Rescuer, Persecutor and Victim (see Figure 7).

EXERCISE 6.3

Identifying your roles in the Drama Game

1. How far and in what ways was your power to live, to successfully relate to other human beings, attacked, forcing you into the role of Victim?

2. How far and in what ways was your power to think, the capacity to understand the world, attacked, forcing you into the role of Victim?

3. How far and in what ways was your power to enjoy yourself, the capacity to experience and make full use of your bodies and emotions, attacked, forcing you into the role of Victim?

4. Who most influenced you in the role of Persecutor? How did this person's (these people's) behaviour make an impression on you?

5. Who most influenced you in the role of Rescuer? How did this person's (these people's) behaviour make an impression on you?

6. How far and in what ways were you allowed to make your own social contacts and your own decisions about who you wanted to be with and when? All such decisions must be appropriate to age.

7. How far were you allowed to know, or protected from knowing, the world? Or allowed or not allowed to come up against situations which would have helped you to understand the world well enough to make decisions about your place in it?

8. How far were you encouraged to learn about yourself? To experience what gave you pleasure? To express how you felt, and how to act upon those feelings?

9. If you are a male, were you encouraged to talk about your feelings? If you are female, were you encouraged to think and to know the world?

10. In your family, who was typically the Persecutor, the Rescuer, and how far were you and the other children the Victims?

11. How far were you emotionally exploited, expected to be totally self-less, always doing things for others, being over-generous and co-operative, and ignoring your own needs?

12. If you are female, how far were you encouraged in the belief that females are inferior to males? If you are male, how far were you encouraged to believe that males are superior to females?

CASE STUDY

James explores his Child

James had been doing self-counselling for around one year, coming to see me whenever he felt the need. His progress through his nurse training was punctuated with bouts of self-doubt. Academically he was fine, but getting in touch with his feelings proved more difficult.

As we explored his upbringing, it transpired that he came from a family where his father was authoritarian, the one who meted out the punishment, and prided himself on 'keeping a well-ordered house, where everybody knows what's what'. Mother was a meek, inoffensive woman who did everything for everybody.

'My inner child?' he asked, closing his eyes, as if in pain, 'stunted, always saying, "yes please," or "did I do that right, dad?"' Through his tears he said, 'I wanted to please him so much, but I never could, or it didn't seem so. I don't think he knew what perfection would look like. He was a hard worker, give him that, and he expected me to be the same.

School work was never a problem, he'd see to that. I never dared miss homework. Play, not much of that – "Education is the thing, my lad. I'll see to that."

'How has it affected me? Too much responsibility too soon, I think. Nothing frivolous or silly in our home. TV strictly regulated, and so on. Now I'm a workaholic, probably still trying to be Mr Perfect. When I go home from the ward it's straight into my books, filling my head with knowledge. I think my Child has been blocked out.'

Together we worked on using imagery to get in touch with his feelings of being a child again. He found this difficult at first, for all he could imagine were re-creations of what actually was. However, he persisted, and after several sessions he was able to 'discover' a new James. It happened in this way.

When I asked him to make contact with his Child, he imagined himself standing in a corner wearing a dunce's hat. Standing over him, waving a stick, but not hitting him, was a scowling, frightening man. Remembering his earlier comment about his abusive teacher, I asked, 'Who is this man?' 'Nobody in particular.' I suggested that perhaps it was a figure to represent all men who fitted the bill of Persecutor.

Noting that his hands moved to cover his abdomen, I said, 'Something seems to be causing you pain. Can you find an image for that?' He visualised an arrow sticking into him. 'So you've been wounded in your abdomen? How can you change that image? I asked. Gradually James was able to change that painful image to one where he was able to deflect the arrow, a bit like Superman. Then, with encouragement, he filled the old wound with healing oil.

Discussion

It is often appropriate to move from one mode of working to another, as in this case, from TA to imagery. James's seeming inability to get in touch with other people's feelings was related to something he said, 'I was always being told to listen, and if I didn't I would be punished in some way. Now I'm listening so hard I miss the meaning.' What James · was saying is that listening is not the same thing as 'paying attention'. Now James was being required to 'listen' at a different level. What was causing the blockage?

His holding his abdomen gave me a clue. The abdomen is the part of the body most closely associated with feelings – when we are distressed our stomach feels out of sorts, for example. The arrow in his stomach pointed to the possibility that he had been very wounded in his emotions, and this could be the blockage.

Changing the image from pain to healing pointed the way for James to continue working on his Child, and as his Child felt it safe to 'feel', so James, the adult, would feel safe to listen to the meaning as well as hearing the words.

SUMMARY

TA offers a simple way of knowing oneself and other people. It is simple because it uses three terms which need little explanation – Parent, Adult and Child. Although TA works very much with the mind, it also draws on feelings and imagery.

Understanding the structure calls for thinking. For example, making sense of the various transactions that can take place between all three ego states draws on a significant level of thinking. At the same time, working with the deeper meanings of the three ego states draws on feelings and imagery. Being able to switch between methods of working is an essential skill in counselling and self-counselling, as we saw in the illustration of James and his Child.

TA is often used in groups – helping people to understand one another. One of the dangers of this is that we can get caught up in identifying and labelling other people's behaviour, in such a way that they feel put down, rather than helped. While understanding other people's behaviour might be a useful by-product of this book, the main thrust is that you should understand more of your own.

The more we recognise our Parent, Adult or Child, and how our behaviour is influencing our relationships, the more we shall help other people to get in touch with their Parent, Adult or Child. Thus your insights benefit not only you, but the wider community of which you are a member.

7
Discovering Person-Centred
Self-Counselling

This chapter is based on the person-centred philosophy of the American psychologist, Carl Rogers. The aim of person-centred counselling is to engage the client in an equal partnership, a philosophy that fits very well into the idea of a partnership between you and your psyche.

The person-centred approach emphasises the capacity and strengths of clients to direct the course and direction of their own therapy. The focus is on entering the client's frame of reference and understanding and tracking precisely what something means to any particular client. Being able to enter the client's frame of reference means active listening and a continual struggle to lay aside preconceptions that would hinder the process. The answers to two basic questions are sought in therapy, 'Who am I?' and 'How can I become myself?' These questions are pertinent for you as self-counsellor.

EVALUATING YOUR PROGRESS

As this is the half-way chapter, now might be an appropriate place to evaluate your progress as a self-counsellor. One way you can judge your progress is how you relate to other people as well as yourself. Rogers identifies seven progressive stages (see Figure 8). Examine all of the stages and decide where you are. You might discover that you have progressed more in some than in others. Realising this will provide impetus for further self-development.

IDENTIFYING THE ESSENTIAL QUALITIES OF BEING PERSON-CENTRED

The remainder of this chapter discusses the essential qualities of the person-centred approach:

● self-acceptance

● self-empathy

Stage 1 Distance from self and others.	<ul><li>Communicates mainly about externals.</li><li>Feelings not owned.</li><li>Ideas viewed in black and white.</li><li>Superficial relationships.</li></ul>
Stage 2 Period of uncertainty and unease.	<ul><li>Intellectualises but does not own feelings.</li><li>Uneasy with subjective experience.</li><li>Reluctant to own problems.</li></ul>
Stage 3 Mainly rigid, but some indication of dawning light.	<ul><li>Uncomfortable remembering past feelings.</li><li>Self kept at a distance.</li><li>Not able to separate self from others.</li><li>Rigid ideas about self.</li><li>Limited acceptance that problems are personal.</li></ul>
Stage 4 The sun has risen, but warmth creates anxiety.	<ul><li>More comfortable describing personal meanings.</li><li>Intense feelings not described in the present.</li><li>Possibility of feelings breaking through causes alarm.</li><li>Unwilling to experience feelings in the present.</li><li>Ideas about self become more free.</li><li>Less rigid thinking.</li></ul>
Stage 5 A period where black and white changes to colour.	<ul><li>Current feelings easier to express.</li><li>More owning of feelings.</li><li>Can handle immediacy of feelings.</li><li>More able to tolerate contradictions and ambiguities.</li><li>Able to question personal meanings and concepts.</li><li>Increased self-responsibility.</li></ul>
Stage 6 Feelings are liberated.	<ul><li>Can accept previously denied feelings and express them.</li><li>Feelings expressed bring liberation.</li><li>More able to work in the present.</li><li>Self is real, not an object.</li></ul>
Stage 7 Living in the present; able to express feelings freely.	<ul><li>Comfortable with what is happening in the present.</li><li>Present feelings experienced with enhanced richness.</li><li>Able to risk expressing feelings.</li></ul>

Fig. 8. Identifying your progress.

- self-genuineness
- self-judgment
- self-regard
- self-warmth.

The internalising of these six qualities is essential in self-counselling for being able to love oneself must precede being able to love other people. A corollary of this is that people who detest themselves invariably hate other people.

Being person-centred is not to be confused with being 'self-centred', which is being engrossed in oneself and one's affairs, usually to the total exclusion of other people. If that is all being person-centred were, then it would be empty and vain.

Being person-centred means recognising yourself as a person of worth, albeit with limitations. At the same time you are not content to remain as you are but are actively involved in trying to make positive changes, changes that will not only affect you but also influence other people for good. You have already moved some way along this road as you have engaged in free association, imagery and the other exercises in the previous chapters.

You may experience difficulty as you attempt to move into a person-centred, reflective way of thinking and feeling. Some people handle the transition very well; others end up feeling that this particular mode is not for them. There was a stage when I said I would give it all up, because of an unfortunate experience with a workshop supervisor, when I felt put-down and totally inept and demoralised. I'm glad I kept on! If you feel like I did, I hope you, too, will keep journeying.

UNDERSTANDING SELF-ACCEPTANCE

To know that we are accepted as we really are, including our strengths and weaknesses, and differences of opinions, no matter how unpleasant or uncongenial, without censure, is a liberating experience. We do not feel accepted unless the very worst in us is accepted too. We never feel accepted when judgement is passed on us.

Our psyche accepts us just as we are, without judgment, even if we don't accept ourselves. So often we work against the psyche by wanting to be someone else, judging ourselves harshly, putting ourselves down, not recognising our good or strong points, but forever concentrating on our weaknesses. That is non-acceptance.

Self-acceptance also means recognising that changes need to be made, and we cannot change something unless we accept it. At the same time, to enter into self-condemnation is fruitless. Condemnation (which lies at the heart of rejection) does not liberate, it oppresses.

We cannot reject ourselves and accept other people. We can only truly accept others when we have already seen, acknowledged and accepted ourselves as we are. Acceptance means we have recognised the gap between the actual and the ideal self, and resolve to try to close the gap. None of us has, or is expected to have, *perfect acceptance*, for that would require a godlike wisdom and an immunity from human frailties.

EXERCISE 7.1

Acceptance and self-awareness

Have a conversation with your psyche and ask your psyche to:

1. identify the parts of yourself you find most difficult to accept

2. identify your behaviours you most need to change

3. show how non-acceptance of yourself interferes in your relationships with others.

UNDERSTANDING SELF-EMPATHY

Empathy means trying to understand the thoughts, feelings, behaviours and personal meanings from either our own or another person's frame of reference.

Accurate empathy is a fragile thing, like a butterfly, beautifully coloured yet so easily damaged. Empathy requires concentration and dedication as you step around your own world. Empathy works with the deeper feelings, the feelings that give substance to the words we use, words that can mean one thing to you and another to me.

It is self-empathy that enables you to plumb the depths of your free association; to feel your way into your imagery. If you had no self-empathy these would be mere intellectual exercises, not living, vibrant experiences of the spirit. The more you learn about yourself, the more you will be able to relate to yourself with accurate empathy.

EXERCISE 7.2

Empathy and self-awareness

Have a conversation with your psyche and ask your psyche to:

1. identify the areas in which you need to learn more about yourself

2. reveal how you can increase your empathy and self-understanding

3. identify the feelings you have most difficulty expressing, and show you what the hindrances are and what changes you can make.

UNDERSTANDING WHAT SELF-GENUINENESS MEANS

Genuineness is the degree to which you are truly yourself, including the way you relate to other people. Genuineness is a sign of integration. Genuineness encourages trust and self-disclosure. It is difficult (if not impossible) for a person to be artificial and open at the same time. Thus in self-counselling, it is essential to be constantly on the look out for areas in which genuineness is being compromised by insincerity.

EXERCISE 7.3

Genuineness and self-awareness

Have a conversation with your psyche, and ask the following questions:

1. What words do you speak that conflict with your feelings?

2. In which relationships are you not genuine?

3. What are you hiding from yourself?

4. In what ways are you not honest with yourself?

CASE STUDY

James confronts a blind spot

James took to heart an observation from his course tutor that he seemed too pleasant a lot of the time in the group; was he being genuine? In a free association session James asked his psyche to show him the truth. The insight that came to James was that he often felt irritated, but that his Christian beliefs led him to cover up his feelings. He discussed this with me, and the conclusion he came to was that his immediate goal would be to find the courage to be open about his feelings, but not to put the other person in the wrong.

UNDERSTANDING SELF-JUDGMENT

Being judgmental of yourself and others hampers self-awareness.

Developing a non-judgmental attitude is an essential quality in self-counselling. When we engage in self-judgment, we dismiss our feelings; we are critical and condemn ourselves, and the criticism and condemnation have their roots in fear, false beliefs and misguided motives. One of these false beliefs is that we should be perfect. The result of self-judgment is that it dulls our self-awareness, divides us from essential parts of ourself, and creates a barrier between us and our psyche.

CASE STUDY

James discovers he is too hard on himself

James (as discussed in Chapter 2) had worked hard on his judgment of other people. At the same time, he was very judgmental of himself. One of the ways he criticised himself was over punctuality. While he could tolerate other people's slack time-keeping, he knew that for him this was something of a virtue, yet it created a great deal of stress for him. He asked his psyche where this came from. He tracked this to his schoolteacher in the infant class, who made all latecomers stand in front of the class and recite, 'I must always come into class on time.' He remembered how anxious he felt in the morning, waiting for his mother to say, 'Now you can go.' He realised that he equated being on time with being a 'good boy'.

EXERCISE 7.4

Judgmentalism and self-awareness

Have a conversation with your psyche, and ask the following questions:

1.   What are the roots of your judgmental attitude?

2.   With whom are you most judgmental?

3.   In what areas of your life are you self-judgmental?

4.   What blind spots do you have recognising your own judgmentalism?

5.   In what areas of your life do you judge others when the same thing is within you?

6.   What do you need to forgive yourself for? This might be one of the roots of your judgmentalism.

UNDERSTANDING SELF-REGARD

People who offer unconditional positive regard help to create a climate which encourages trust and openness. It is where we communicate a deep and genuine caring, not filtered through our own feelings, thoughts and behaviours.

On the other hand, conditional regard implies enforced control, and compliance with behaviour dictated by someone else. Self-regard means that we relate to ourselves with the same degree of genuine caring, in much the same way as we demonstrate acceptance towards ourselves.

EXERCISE 7.5

Regard and self-awareness

Have a conversation with your psyche, and ask the following questions:

1. How far are you appropriately concerned about your own welfare?

2. In what ways do you not appreciate yourself?

3. In what ways do you affirm that you are a worthwhile person?

4. In what ways do you indulge in unfair criticism of yourself?

5. If you were someone else, how far would you feel safe with yourself?

6. In what ways do you feel unable to be free to be yourself?

7. How far can you trust your feelings about yourself?

8. In what ways do you knowingly hurt yourself?

UNDERSTANDING SELF-WARMTH

A question to be asked, as in all the six qualities, is, can you express warmth to someone else if you do not feel warmth towards yourself? I would come down with full weight on 'No'. This would be like a fountain sending out both hot and cold water from the same spout.

Warmth is genuine and springs from an attitude of feeling comfortable with oneself. If you cannot be friends with yourself, how can you show friendliness to others? Warmth is like a fluffy hot water bottle on a cold night.

EXERCISE 7.6

Warmth and self-awareness

Have a conversation with your psyche, and ask the following questions:

1. With whom do you not respond with warmth and interest?

2. In what circumstances is your warmth conditional on how you feel towards people?

3. How far is your warmth towards someone dependent on the other person showing you warmth?

4. How is your warmth towards someone affected by that person's criticism of you?

5. How would you rate your warmth towards yourself – high, medium or low?

6. Is your warmth towards others genuine or is it only for self-gain?

CASE STUDY

James turns everything into a joke

By nature James was an outgoing man, and very warm. He smiled a lot, and was invariably bright and cheery. He was good to be with. One of his traits, to which he wryly admitted when I pointed it out to him, was to turn almost everything into a joke. While it was not my intention to 'wipe the smile off his face', it had that effect. He said he would have to work on it. This is what he later said.

'What you said really made an impression. Why did I do it? I took myself off to my room and had a free association session, and started with that word, 'joke'. I tracked it back to my mother. When dad was getting at me, mum would take me aside, when he'd gone, and say, "Don't let him see you're upset, son. Try and find something to joke about. Your dad likes that."

'I think I must have been about ten. I remembered (the first time I'd thought about that) when he was going on about my writing. In my memory he looked terrifying. Although I didn't feel like it, I remember starting to giggle, and pointing at my writing, I said, "It looks like a spider's crawled over the page." Mum laughed, and then so did he. It worked! I'd found a safe way of gaining approval. But I'm not being genuine, am I?'

SUMMARY

In all your self-counselling, your psyche will never betray you, judge or criticise you, even though you may do all these things to yourself. The person-centred approach emphasises the capacity and strengths of clients to direct the course and direction of their own therapy. The concept of self-actualisation is at the centre of person-centred therapy, so it seems a natural progression to think of these concepts applied to self-counselling.

It is worth pointing out that using free association and imagery are very person-centred skills, for only as you are able to get into your own inner world can you make sense of them. Throughout this book the co-operation between you and your psyche is stressed, in much the same way as the relationship between the person-centred counsellor and the client is established and maintained.

The idea of relating to yourself in this way might seem foreign, and too difficult. It might seem too woolly, and vague. You may prefer something more structured, more related to techniques, yet perhaps this is the very area your psyche is directing you to work on; to get away from structure and trust yourself to the unknown. But already you have worked with some of the principles, for as you dialogue with your psyche you are learning to be person-centred.

8
Understanding Body, Mind and Spirit

Self-counselling is about working towards wholeness. To attend to the body and neglect the mind and spirit would be like creating just the shell of a building. To concentrate on the mind and ignore the body and the spirit would be like creating a living computer. To concentrate on the spirit and ignore the body and the mind would create an angel, not a human being.

To be wholly human, we must accept all three — body, mind and spirit — and cherish each, for each depends on and interacts with the other. The body helps us make sense of the world; the mind tells us what something is; and the spirit interprets our feelings.

LEARNING HOW TO ATTEND TO YOUR INNER DIALOGUE

Speaking to oneself is considered by some to be the first sign of madness. Yet we all speak to ourselves in what we call 'inner dialogue', even though we might not be aware of actually 'speaking'. I would like to propose that the psyche is constantly communicating with us. Sometimes we don't hear that inner voice; sometimes we hear and do not respond; sometimes we hear and ignore.

Just as communication between two people can be difficult, so can the inner dialogue we have with our psyche. Free association, imagery and dreams are three ways in which you have already started to converse with your psyche.

When we listen carefully to our inner self, we are more able to express thoughts and feelings more clearly.

EXERCISE 8.1

Letting your psyche speak to you

1.   Taking any of the free association, or imagery, trigger words in the Appendix (pages 120 and 125), start a conversation with your psyche.

2. You may imagine your psyche sitting opposite you, or at the other end of a telephone, or however you feel most comfortable.

3. You may discover that your conversation moves into free association, imagery and the use of symbols.

LEARNING TO TRUST YOUR PSYCHE

'Do you trust your psyche?' This might not be an easy question to answer, for it demands openness and honesty. Don't be afraid of offending your psyche! You might like to use this as one of your conversations. Above all, try to remember that your psyche is all-knowing, full of wisdom, with no limitations of education, culture or language. The psyche transcends the limitations of our consciousness, and accesses the timelessness of the collective unconscious.

Why is it then that we find it difficult to listen to our psyche, our inner self? Part of the answer lies in the fact that if we heard, we might have to change how we think, feel or behave. Perhaps our inner ears are deaf to the message. We need to trust the psyche, and believe that the psyche will never harm us; rather, the psyche brings healing. If the message is unpalatable, then we must face it. Not until we have will we be able to move forward.

EXERCISE 8.2

Identifying your inner interference factors

1. When conversing with your inner self, be attentive, be patient, and don't interrupt the message.

2. Remove outer distractions before conversing with your inner self, or as they occur.

3. Tiredness, tension and hunger all interfere with accurate listening to the inner self.

4. The psyche will constantly challenge your preconceived ideas, prejudices, assumptions, rigid thinking; all of which interfere with accurate listening.

5. The psyche is all-wise, so when it reveals something to you, don't shoot it down as not being relevant.

RELATING TO YOUR BODY

Part of being self-aware means being aware of the body and of its relationship with the mind and the spirit. Care of the body, without becoming body-bound, is essential for good health.

For most of the time we are unaware of our body, until something, such as pain, draws our attention to it. Some functions are within our control, such as the muscles of movement, but *how* they function remains outside our control.

Other organs, such as the brain and the endocrine system, function completely at an unconscious level, although some systems of mind control, such as Yoga, can exert a surprising influence even on the deeper systems of the body.

When a computer is attacked by a virus, strange and distressing things happen. So it is with any disease that attacks the body – which is more complex than any computer. Indeed the body is so wonderfully constructed that something as insignificant as a pinprick sends messages to all parts of the body, and in some way, all parts are affected by it.

The eye is more than a window letting light in and allowing us to see. The eye expresses knowledge, character, attitude, inclination, opinion, passion, and many other emotions. The eye is a good barometer of the inner thoughts.

Hearing involves the whole self. We can regard the whole body being engaged and concentrated on hearing whatever is being spoken. Figuratively the ear can be open or closed.

The heart is one of the three principal focal points of the body (the other two are the brain and the sexual organs). The heart is more than a pump pushing blood around the body – symbolically it is the seat of affection. The blood carries life-giving oxygen through the body, and potentially destructive carbon dioxide away. Without adequate blood supply to all parts of the body, organs will die.

We only become aware of breathing when something is not functioning properly. Breathing and the circulation of the blood function together, and difficulty in breathing may symbolise difficulty in assimilating the principles of the spirit. Inhalation and exhalation are also symbolic of the ebb and flow of the tides, and of the rhythm of the universe.

EXERCISE 8.3

Exploring your body

1. Find a quiet place, free from distractions.

2. Spend time allowing your psyche to scan your body.

3. Ask your psyche, 'Is there any part of my body you want me to become aware of? Is there any part of my body I dislike or am not happy with?' Remember, if you do not like a part of your body, you do not like yourself.

4. Ask your psyche to show you how you can change dislike to love.

IDENTIFYING THE FACULTIES OF THE MIND

In general terms, the mind enables us to think, feel and take action. It is the seat of the intelligence and of memory. With the mind we perceive, remember, acquire knowledge, consider, evaluate, and make decisions. The mind is concerned with sensations, emotions, desires, various types of reasoning, motives, choices, traits of personality, and the unconscious.

acquisitiveness	decisiveness	judgment	self-esteem
affiliation	destructiveness	language	sensation
aggression	determination	love	thinking
awe	feelings	memory	time
caution	hope	musicality	wisdom
colour	idealism	numbers	wit
concentration	mimicry	order	wonder
conscientiousness	individuality	perception	word association
practicality	intuition	secretiveness	

Fig. 9. Some of the faculties of the mind.

EXERCISE 8.4

Identifying your mind faculties

1. Choose any of the faculties listed in Figure 9, and, using free association, find out where your psyche takes you.

2. Along the way you may also like to use imagery to explore any of the avenues into which your psyche takes you.

3. This is not an exercise to hurry through.

UNDERSTANDING THE MIND–BODY RELATIONSHIP

The mind and body are so closely related that the body often becomes the focus of psychosomatic problems. The term 'psychosomatic' comes from the Greek *psyche*, meaning 'spirit' or 'soul', and *soma*, meaning 'body', and refers to the effect of the mind on the body's health. Repeated emotional stress stimulates the involuntary nervous system and the glands of internal secretion, and can cause dysfunction or structural damage in the body's tissues and organs.

Examples of the mind–body interaction

The interplay between mind and body is very sensitive. However, it must never be assumed that any illness is 'all in the mind', to be dismissed as unimportant. The pain, for example, is every bit as real as if it were from a broken leg. Never assume that self-awareness does away with the need for the services of your doctor.

1. Chronic tension headaches often progress to chronic back pain, which can become disabling.

2. Emotional stress can arise from particular life events, such as the death of a loved one, divorce, job loss or illness. Although this type of stress may be of shorter duration than 'everyday' stress, it can be more severe and cause greater physical damage.

3. Other ailments which may be psychosomatic include:

   ● high blood pressure (hypertension)
   ● peptic ulcers
   ● bronchial asthma
   ● migraine headaches
   ● ulcerative colitis
   ● insomnia
   ● skin diseases
   ● allergies.

UNDERSTANDING THE SPIRIT

What is spirituality? And is it different from being 'religious'? How this is understood would depend on the meaning of the word 'spirit'. It may mean the Holy Spirit; it may also mean the finer perceptions of life.

Jung's view of the 'spirit' is that it is the non-material aspect of humans, and the opposite of matter. But spirit cannot be described or defined, for it is infinite, spaceless, formless and without image. The spirit is 'other-worldly', not of this world; it is not limited by creeds or beliefs.

Roberto Assagioli (founder of Psychosynthesis) speaks of the 'higher self'; not a part of ego; above and beyond self. Psychosynthesis bridges body, mind and spirit.

EXERCISE 8.5

Exploring body, mind and spirit

1. Get yourself into a relaxed state; concentrate on your breathing, and let all tension go.

2. Let your inner eye scan your body and pick up any areas of tension. Don't simply look at the outer body, become aware of the inner organs too.

3. Ask your psyche what that tension is telling you.

4. Concentrate on your mind. A useful way to do this is to imagine you are watching a video tape. Don't analyse, just view. If you find your mind racing, or you feel anxious, stay with the feeling, don't fight it. One way of controlling a racing mind is to imagine yourself running. Feel the exertion, then gradually slow the pace to a quick trot, then a slow jog, then a quick walk. Let the walk become gradually slower until you sit down. By now your mind will start to feel rested.

5. Concentrate on such words as love, wisdom, serenity, peace, light, spirit, affection.

6. Let your psyche show you how each word you dwell on influences your body, mind and spirit.

7. When you have finished, you might find it helpful to write up your thoughts and feelings.

8. In all the exercises in which you work with the psyche, don't forget to say thank you.

CASE STUDY

James explores neglect

About 18 months into his training, James found himself becoming short-tempered with his family. Little things became major issues. He put this down to 'exam nerves'. But when he passed his first year exams, and he knew he should therefore have relaxed, he was still tense. Strange dreams (which he didn't bother to record!) disturbed his sleep and he went off his food.

In one of his dreams (which he did record) he found himself in an area of rebuilding. All around were half-demolished houses, brick rubble and chaos. He entered a run-down house. The window frames were chipped, glass was broken, the front door was hanging from its hinges. Cobwebs were everywhere. An old-fashioned, embroidered, framed motto hung lopsided on a wall. It had only three words – 'The Unseen Guest'. Jenny shook him awake. He was sobbing and shaking.

This was no ordinary dream, so at the first opportunity he devoted his time to a free association session. He asked a question: 'Why was that house so neglected?' His memory took him back to his Sunday School teacher. He pictured her small sitting room. Upon one wall hung an embroidered text which read, 'Christ is the unseen Guest at every meal, the unseen Listener at every conversation.' The same feeling of grief that had troubled his dream overtook him. He knew why. He was that house.

Some time into his training he had stopped his regular worship with the family, making as his excuse his mountain of study. Soon he had stopped going at all. He knew that he had neglected his spiritual life, and this neglect had spilled over and affected his body and his mind. Discovering this, he could do something to remedy the situation.

SUMMARY

Self-counselling is working towards wholeness, and part of that is becoming aware of the relationship between body, mind and spirit. Neglect of one will affect the other two. Mind, body and spirit are inseparable; they influence, and are dependent on, one another for full functioning. The mind cannot function on its own; it needs the body. The mind influences the body; and dysfunction of the mind-body relationship may produce psychosomatic illnesses.

The spirit part of humans is non-material, and is not to be confused with mere religious expression, although that is part of it. Spirituality is to do with growth, harmony and striving for potential.

In order to be aware of the trinity of body, mind and spirit, we need to develop that inner awareness that tells us when something is amiss. You can use periods of relaxation to become more aware of your inner self. If part of your body is feeling tense, it could mean that this is expressing a tension of the mind or spirit. If your mind is in a whirl, it could be that you have been neglecting your body. If, as James discovered, your spiritual life has been neglected, the other two parts of you join in the feeling. Listening to any one of the three can lead you into awareness of deeper issues in your life. But having become aware, you must do something with the revelation. Not to take action is an insult to yourself.

9
Learning to Work with your Personality

There are many approaches to the study of personality, a subject which has occupied philosophers and psychologists for generations. Carl Jung, in his *Psychological Types*, proposes six preferences of personality – extraversion and introversion; sensing and intuition; thinking and feeling.

Isabel Briggs-Myers in *Gifts Differing* extends Jung's work to include judgment and perception, thus giving four dimensions with eight preferences (see Figure 10). For readers who would like to add to their understanding of personality typing, *Please Understand Me*, by David Keirsey and Marilyn Bates, provides a detailed self-scoring questionnaire.

- Extraversion/Introversion is the way we relate to the world around us.

- Sensing/Intuition is the way we perceive the world.

- Thinking/Feeling is the way we make judgments.

- Judgment/Perception is the way we make decisions.

EXPLORING THE EIGHT PREFERENCES OF PERSONALITY

Extraversion (E)
People who are more extraverted than introverted:

- are generally sociable and outgoing

- relate to people and things around them

- endeavour to make their decisions in agreement with other people

- are interested in variety and in working with people

- may become impatient with long, slow tasks

- do not mind being interrupted by people

- are usually relaxed and confident

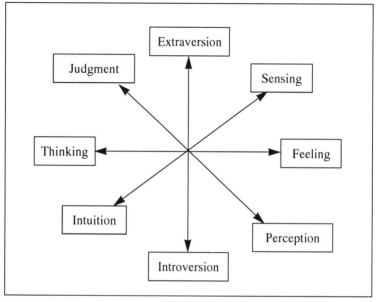

Fig. 10. Personality preferences.

- are usually people of action

- tend to be practical achievers

- feel more at home doing than with ideas.

Introversion (I)

People who are more introverted than extraverted:

- prefer making decisions independently of other people

- tend to be quiet, diligent at working alone

- tend to be socially reserved

- dislike being interrupted while working

- are liable to forget names and faces

- tend to be reserved and questioning

- are interested in what is happening within themselves

- are good at the abstract and ideas

- tend to bottle up feelings

- tend not to be very practical.

EXERCISE 9.1

Assessing your E/I

1. From the descriptions given above, would you rate yourself more E than I, or vice versa?

2. In what circumstances do you rely more on the other preference?

Sensing (S)

People who are more sensing than intuitive:

● prefer what is concrete, real, factual, structured, tangible, here-and-now

● tend to mistrust their intuition

● think in careful, detail-by-detail accuracy

● are very observant

● remember real facts, and make few errors of fact

● may possibly miss a grasp of the overall

● tend to be lovers of pleasure; love life

● live in and for the present

● can be accused of being frivolous

● are very conscientious

● are not comfortable using imagination.

Intuition (N)

People who have more intution than sensing:

● prefer possibilities, theories, patterns, the overall, inventions, and the new

● become bored with the nitty-gritty details, the concrete and actual

● need facts to relate to concepts

● think and discuss in spontaneous leaps of intuition

● are not very observant of detail

● find problem-solving comes easily

● may show a tendency to make errors of fact

● crave inspiration and the novel

- are very imaginative
- tend to be restless and always seeking out something new.

EXERCISE 9.2

Assessing your S/N

1. From the descriptions given above, would you rate yourself more S than N, or vice versa?
2. In what circumstances do you rely on the other preference?

Thinking (T)
People with more thinking than feeling (head types):

- make judgments about life, people, occurrences and things based on logic, analysis and hard evidence
- avoid irrationality, sentiment, and decisions based on feelings and values
- are interested in logic, analysis and verifiable conclusions
- are less comfortable with empathy, value and personal warmth
- may step on others' feelings and needs without realising it
- often neglect to take into consideration the values of others
- are often considered impersonal
- are more likely to believe that their decisions are right and other people's wrong
- tend to be businesslike rather than friendly
- are often more truthful than tactful.

Feeling (F)
People with more feeling than thinking (heart types):

- make judgments about life, people, occurrences, and things based on empathy, warmth and personal values
- are more interested in people and feelings than in impersonal logic, analysis and things
- regard conciliation and harmony as more important than being on top or achieving impersonal goals

- get along with people in general
- are usually strong in social skills
- often find it difficult to be businesslike
- are generally good talkers, but may ramble
- often find it difficult to work to a structure
- tend to consider feeling superior to thinking
- often more tactful than truthful.

EXERCISE 9.3

Assessing your T/F

1. From the descriptions given above, would you rate yourself more T than F, or vice versa?

2. In what circumstances do you rely more on the other preferences?

Judgment (J)
People with more judgment than perception:

- are decisive, firm and sure
- like setting goals and sticking to them
- want to make decisions, and get on to the next project
- will leave an unfinished project behind and go on to new tasks and not look back, if that's what has to be done
- give priority to work over play
- are good at meeting deadlines
- tend to be judgmental of themselves and other people
- tend not to like the unexpected
- like to get things settled and out of the way
- tend to think they know what other people should do.

Perception (P)
People who have more perception than judgment:

- always want to know more before making decisions and judgments

- are open, flexible, adaptive, non-judgmental

- are able to appreciate all sides of an issue

- always welcome new perspectives and new information about issues

- are difficult to pin down

- hate working to deadlines

- are often so indecisive and noncommittal that they frustrate themselves and other people

- are often involved in many tasks

- give priority to play rather than work

- often need to be forced into making a decision.

EXERCISE 9.4

Assessing your J/P

1. From the descriptions given above, would you rate yourself more J than P, or vice versa?

2. In what circumstances do you rely more on the other preference?

CASE STUDY

Susan identifies her type

When Susan (whom you met in Chapter 5) did the Kiersey and Bates' assessment, she came out as INFJ – Introverted, Intuitive, Feeling and Judgment (see Figure 11). She summed herself up thus:

1. I'm not very outgoing, unless I have to be, but too much takes a lot out of me. (E/I)

2. My sensing is very low. I'm ham-fisted and not at all practical. (S/N)

3. Although I came out F, I'm also a thinker, and there wasn't much to choose between them. I use my F relating to people, and that sometimes gives the impression that I'm more extraverted than I really am. (T/F)

4. I'm pretty determined, and don't easily give up. (J/P)

5.   My P is low and I wish I could let go a bit more and play. (J/P)

Susan realised that her low S was a disadvantage. For example, she could not sew or knit, at anything above a very basic level. She enrolled for evening classes in dressmaking, and much to her surprise, did very well. But there was an unexpected spin-off. While she was cutting out a dress, out of the blue she knew why she had never been interested in sewing. Her mother (an accomplished seamstress) always belittled Susan's childish attempts to sew. So in the end she gave up, telling herself that she couldn't do it.

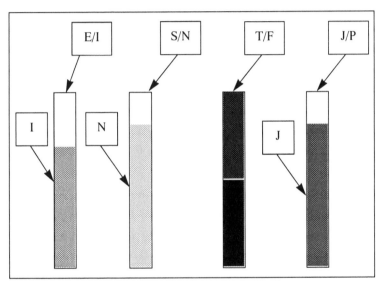

Fig. 11 — Susan's presentation of her personality type.

EXERCISE 9.5

Applying preferences to self-counselling
The majority of us are a mixture of all preferences; self-counselling makes use of all eight preferences.

E/L: You need enough I to be able to make emotional contact with your inner world, yet enough E not to get so caught up in introspection that you lose touch with reality, but not so much that it interferes with listening to yourself. The E part of you may feel under pressure to do all the self-talking. The I part may feel ignored if your self-talk doesn't leave time for reflection.

S/N: You need enough **N** to work with free association and imagery, yet enough **S** to keep you firmly rooted in the present, yet not so much that you start quarrelling with yourself over minutiae. The **S** part of you may feel irritated by your **N** when it jumps to conclusions without working through obvious stages. The **N** part may feel irritated by **S** which urges carefulness and caution.

T/F: You need enough **F** to relate to yourself with empathy, yet enough **T** to be able to analyse what is going on, and to keep your mind in some order, yet not so much as to reject feelings because you cannot understand them. The **T** part of you may feel irritated by the **F** wanting to concentrate on feelings. The **F** part may feel irritated by **T** who insists on analysing everything logically before making a judgment.

J/P: You need enough **P** to use imagery and free association, and make contact with the parts of yourself that are childlike, yet enough **J** to show the way through the woods, and create a structure. The **J** part may feel irritated by the **P** which never seems to be able to make a decision and never wants to get down to serious business. The **P** part may feel irritated by the **J** which concentrates on structure, and won't let things just happen.

Balance between two parts of any dimension is essential; and **integration** of all eight is something to aim for.

Question
In working through this chapter, how far do you see your own preferences influencing your study of self-counselling?

CASE STUDY

Sheila and Maggie arrange a meeting

Sheila and Maggie are business partners. Sheila's type is **ENFJ**; Maggie's is **ESTJ**. They arranged a meeting to discuss their plan for the following year. Sheila gave it some thought, jotted a few ideas down on the back of an envelope, and waited for things to bubble away in her subconscious.

Sheila arrived promptly at Maggie's house, carrying a bundle of papers and books she thought they might look at. Maggie, on the other hand, had meticulously prepared a programme, with everything spread in strict order around the table. A neatly drawn flowchart indicated the expected route of the discussion.

When they had been going for a few minutes, Maggie said something that caught Sheila's attention, and reminded her of something among her papers. Maggie asked her to keep that until later: 'It'll throw me off my stride. Can't deal with tangents.'

Maggie made notes as she went along, neatly appending them to her programme. Several times she picked out a diagram from her collection to illustrate a point. All her drawings and overhead transparencies were numbered and kept in strict order.

Several times Sheila said something like, 'What do you think they will feel about that?' to which Maggie replied, 'If it's presented logically, they can't really argue, can they?'

After Maggie had covered all the points, Sheila said, 'Maggie, I've written this article for the Journal, will you proofread it for me? I know you'll dot the i's and cross the t's.' Maggie agreed.

Maggie said, 'I need to think through an idea, here it is, what does it look like to you? What will the staff think about it?'

Discussion of Sheila and Maggie

1. Sheila and Maggie matched their **E** and **J**. Both liked working with people and were outgoing and worked well to deadlines.

2. Maggie perceived the world through her **S** and worked well with detail and needed to take her plan in a logical sequence.

3. Sheila perceived the world through her **N** and would have been quite happy to let things roll and see what developed.

4. **S** and **T** often go together. Maggie, though not insensitive to feelings, was more comfortable using logic to achieve her goal. Sheila needed to take other people's feelings into account.

5. Maggie needed Sheila's **N** and **F**; Sheila needed Maggie's **S** and **T**.

SUMMARY

The study of personality is complex and rather than try to cover the whole gamut of theories, only one was presented – that of Carl Jung's preferences as they were developed by Isabel Briggs-Myers.

While the majority of us do function better with certain preferences rather than others, every one of us needs all eight to perform at our optimum.

- People who are too extraverted often get on people's nerves; someone who is too introverted often has difficulty making contact with people at all.

- People who are high on sensing can get so caught up in counting the trees that they miss the beauty of the wood; people who are too intuitive often seem 'away with the fairies'.

- People who are too high on thinking often intellectualise everything; people who are too high on feeling often swamp others by their warmth.

- People who are too high on judgment often become judge, jury and executioner; people who are too high on perception often give the impression of being grown up children.

Effective self-counselling might require you to work towards making changes in the way you relate to the world; how you perceive the world; the way you make judgments; and the way you make decisions. Even small changes can work wonders.

10
Focusing on Change

Self-counselling, inevitably, involves change. Change can be uncomfortable – for you and for other people, who have come to know you as you are. But if self-counselling does not produce some change, then of what use is it?

Self-awareness is to do with discovering and accepting the fact that we are unique. But, as with all aspects of self-awareness, if our insights remain locked up within us they are of little benefit. The miser might have stacks of gold, but if he does not use it, of what use is it? So with the insights you gain – use them, for yourself and for the benefit of others.

IDENTIFYING YOUR UNIQUE SELF

Accepting your uniqueness means that you accept yourself. This was discussed under acceptance in Chapter 7. But just as we have both a *need* and a *right* to have our uniqueness respected by others, so we must respect ourselves for who we are. When we respect our uniqueness, we feel we understand ourselves; and when we do that, there is more chance that other people will understand us too.

In the process of self-awareness, the psyche's light will undoubtedly reveal dark areas of our life, which we need to change if we are to move forward. Part of the purpose of this book is to help you appreciate your good points, and yet work to changing the not so good points so that you can accept your unique self.

ASSESSING YOUR PERSONALITY PREFERENCES AND CHANGE

This section extends the discussion introduced in the previous chapter, by relating personality preferences to change. In all personality work, it is unwise to say, 'this is'; rather we should say, 'this is what might be'. Bearing this in mind, the following possibilities are suggested.

Extraverts	Introverts
The **E** part of us will accept change with enthusiasm, mainly because change brings with it the possibility of new relationships. If anything, the extravert may rush into change with open arms before counting the cost.	The **I** part of us proceeds with caution. Change for the introvert brings more questions than answers, and that is unsettling.
Sensing	**Intuition**
The **S** part of us resists change, because it disturbs the status quo. When the **S** part cannot find the next logical piece in the plan, there is anxiety. **S** needs to know what is, to have hands on.	The **N** part of us enjoys possibilities, revels in the unknown, and new beginnings. **N** is creative. Change energises.
Thinking	**Feeling**
T asks is it 'true or false'. Analysis requires time, so if change is hurried, before the logic is fully accepted, it will produce stress and will be rejected.	**F** asks is it 'agreeable or disagreeable'. Change is acceptable provided there is sufficient attention paid to the 'human' aspect, and that there is ample time for discussion.
Judgment	**Perception**
The **J** part excels in plans, decisions and conclusions. If change is protracted by people who can't make up their minds, stress is likely to occur.	The **P** part puts off making decisions. Open-mindedness is a **P** strength. Putting perceptive people under pressure, *eg* with deadlines, will create stress.

EXERCISE 10.1

Assessing your unique self

1. Answer by prefixing each pair of values with, I am more ... than I am ...

2. Place an X in one of the boxes between each pair of values.

3. When you have answered all the questions, connect all the Xs to give your profile.

Affectionate	❏	❏	❏	❏	❏	Cold
Arrogant	❏	❏	❏	❏	❏	Modest
Agreeable	❏	❏	❏	❏	❏	Contradictory
Boring	❏	❏	❏	❏	❏	Interesting
Compassionate	❏	❏	❏	❏	❏	Severe
Conventional	❏	❏	❏	❏	❏	Modern
Dominant	❏	❏	❏	❏	❏	Passive
Easy-going	❏	❏	❏	❏	❏	Demanding

Exacting	❏	❏	❏	❏	❏	Tolerant
Friendly	❏	❏	❏	❏	❏	Aloof
Hesitant	❏	❏	❏	❏	❏	Adventurous
Happy	❏	❏	❏	❏	❏	Sad
Hard	❏	❏	❏	❏	❏	Sensitive
Impulsive	❏	❏	❏	❏	❏	Cautious
Introvert	❏	❏	❏	❏	❏	Extravert
Insecure	❏	❏	❏	❏	❏	Secure
Industrious	❏	❏	❏	❏	❏	Lazy
Intellectual	❏	❏	❏	❏	❏	Practical
Inattentive	❏	❏	❏	❏	❏	Attentive
Imaginative	❏	❏	❏	❏	❏	Dull
Incompetent	❏	❏	❏	❏	❏	Competent
Lively	❏	❏	❏	❏	❏	Quiet
Light-hearted	❏	❏	❏	❏	❏	Serious
Moody	❏	❏	❏	❏	❏	Stable
Mature	❏	❏	❏	❏	❏	Immature
Mean	❏	❏	❏	❏	❏	Generous
Open	❏	❏	❏	❏	❏	Secretive
Pessimistic	❏	❏	❏	❏	❏	Optimistic
Patient	❏	❏	❏	❏	❏	Impatient
Rigid	❏	❏	❏	❏	❏	Flexible
Reliable	❏	❏	❏	❏	❏	Unreliable
Submissive	❏	❏	❏	❏	❏	Assertive
Self-confident	❏	❏	❏	❏	❏	Unsure
Shy	❏	❏	❏	❏	❏	Sociable
Tense	❏	❏	❏	❏	❏	Relaxed
Unattractive	❏	❏	❏	❏	❏	Likeable
Unresolved	❏	❏	❏	❏	❏	Persistent
Unaspiring	❏	❏	❏	❏	❏	Ambitious

When you have created your profile, ask someone who knows you very well to comment on how accurately you know yourself.

EXERCISE 10.2

Assessing your change rating

1. On a scale 1–10, how would you rate your attitude towards change, where 'unwelcome' is 1 and 'welcome' is 10?

2. How far do you think this attitude is influenced by your personality preferences as outlined above?

3. Are there any current situations where you are finding change difficult, and how could your understanding of personality help you in facing that change?

INTRODUCING A FOUR-STAGE MODEL OF CHANGE

Change might be uncomfortable, even scary. Change, when forced upon us, is invariably resisted, and frequently sabotaged. The change involved in self-counselling is embraced because it is self-initiated. This does not mean that it is less scary; indeed, it could be said to be more frightening because we are controlling it.

The model presented below has been inspired by Gerard Egan's decision-making model, and modified with self-counselling specifically in mind. You may become aware that there is something in your life you need to change, but cannot see how. Breaking the problem down is a logical way of making progress.

The four stages are:

1. focusing on **alternatives** for action

2. focusing on the **consequences** of the alternatives

3. focusing on **priorities** of the alternative consequences

4. focusing on **criteria** – the rules by which you select a single alternative or a set of alternatives on the basis of their preferred consequences.

The experience of change can be difficult to the extent that any one of the four elements is defective; for example when:

1. The search for alternatives is incomplete.

2. Important consequences are overlooked.

3. The values are not recognised or dismissed.

4. Superficial criteria are chosen.

Points to remember

1. Important decisions should generally be for the common good.

2. Too many important decisions are based on attraction rather than on accurate data. Some of the factors that influence attraction are:

● biases and prejudices

● conflict and rivalry between what you want and what you need

● panic

● beliefs and traditions that no longer serve any useful purpose

- wanting to comply with other people's demands of you
- your inner Child seeking approval.

Backing a tug of war team

One way of helping to resolve conflicts is to construct a tug of war.

1. The rope is the problem.

2. One team is For, the other is Against.

3. Label each person in both teams with a particular part of the problem.

4. Then, using your imagination, engage the two teams, and watch which side 'wins'.

5. This might not be scientific, but it can be fun!

Assessing your intention to change

Your intention to change is influenced by:

- wanting to take charge of your own life

- not wasting time and energy blaming other people or circumstances for your problems

- refusing to capitulate to unfavourable odds

- having a sense of direction in your life

- being versatile – thinking about and creating options

- being involved in the world of other people

- being able to evaluate your goals against the needs and wants of other people

- being ready to work for win-win rather than win-lose situations

- having a repertoire of actions, thoughts and behaviour to help you cope with changes.

CASE STUDY

Carol is in a mess

Carol is a mature student nurse, speaking to the college counsellor. Carol says, 'I'm in a mess. I moved out of the hospital residence six months ago into a house with four other students, several miles from the college, so I had to buy a car. Two of the others have moved on since then, and the two new ones are awful. They leave the kitchen like a pig sty, and we have endless rows. The atmosphere is so unpleasant. Plus the fact that they're so noisy, loud music and banging doors.

'A month ago I had an accident with the car, when it was outside in the street. I've only got third party, so I couldn't claim on the insurance, and it's going to cost a packet to repair. I'm already badly overdrawn and the bank keep writing to me. They take off so much when my pay cheque goes in that I barely have enough to live on. In fact I eat so badly that I'm losing weight like an anorexic. To crown it all, my last project at college was awful. They made me resubmit, and I can't find the energy to even start it. What am I going to do?'

Using the four-stage model
The counsellor helps Carol to use the four-stage model.

1. Focusing on alternatives
Carol says to the counsellor, 'I could call a "house meeting" to talk about the difficulties and as a group establish some ground rules. I could ask for an interview with the bank manager to explain my situation. I could speak to my tutor and ask for more time.'

2. Focusing on consequences.
Carol says to the counsellor, 'I most definitely do not want to move back into residence, for it felt as if I was trapped in a cell. So staying where I am is important to me. I think I could speak to some of the others about calling a meeting, but I'm not sure how to go about that. I'd like some help with that, please. I quite like the other girls, if only they could control their noise. I know that my overdraft is mainly caused by the expenses of the car. Perhaps I don't really need it. Since I bought it, a new bus service has started that would take me to the hospital, for most of the time at least. I used to enjoy cycling, so I could think about that. I don't like confronting the bank manager, so would like to rehearse that before I see him. As for my project, I think by pulling out all the stops I can get finished on time.'

3. Focusing on priorities
Carol decides to: get the project done on time; speak to the bank manager, and possibly take some agency work during the holidays; improve the house atmosphere; see if she can manage without the car.

4. Focusing on criteria

Carol says to the counsellor, 'My project is not really the problem I thought it was. Talking things over seems to have released some of the trapped energy, and I already have some material and lots of ideas. I want you to help me rehearse talking to the bank manager. I also would like you to help me to examine my finances and see if together we can come up with some suggestions to put to the bank manager. I also want to do some assertive rehearsal with you, so that when I do get the girls together, I'll be able to say what I want without losing my temper. When I work with the finances I'm going to look very carefully at the car, and see if I can manage without it. I'm going to give myself three months trial on public transport, before making a final decision about it, though at this stage I think there's a strong possibility that I'll get rid of it; it's causing me too much hassle.'

SUMMARY

Change is seldom easy or simple. Even small changes often bring unexpected consequences. Change seldom involves just you, or one person. Change in one person's life impinges on the lives of many other people. Growth and self-awareness are changes, and while they may benefit us, other people have to accommodate to what has, or is, taking place in our lives. People on the periphery of our lives are not so affected as those close to us. When one partner in a relationship, for example, is caught up in self-development change, tensions can be created because the old familiar ground is no longer common to them.

Thus change requires much acceptance and accommodation from others, yet at the same time, it requires patience and self-understanding on your part too. Things that were once essential to you may assume less importance, and vice versa. If you find that change brings you into conflict with parts of yourself, then this is an indication that you have work yet to do to resolve the conflict. If you find yourself in conflict with someone else, likewise there is work still to do. Part of your overall change might be to work towards resolution with someone else, and in that, you might find that you have helped someone else along the road to change.

11
Working with Beliefs and Values

A belief is a conviction that some statement, being, thing or phenomenon is true, although we have no conclusive proof. We only say we *believe* that something is the case when we cannot claim to prove that it is.

In religion, belief is based on acceptance of the reported existence, acts and teachings of religious figures, not witnessed first-hand but passed down the generations in written form and ritual. Cultural beliefs help us to make sense of non-material ideas such as spirituality and the world of the universe.

Values are the principles or standards which guide a person or society. Values are what we judge are valuable and important in life, or what we consider good or beneficial to our well-being. Values are learned beliefs, largely culturally determined, which show in our attitudes. As enduring beliefs, values are part of our personality, and direct how we behave and think and, therefore, influence how we feel.

Values may be personal, such as honour, truth, freedom, education, the right to work, equality, the worth of life, doing what is right, and not doing what is wrong, justice and fairness, and honesty. These cannot be bought or sold, things can. Gold is an example of something we value, as is money, to which we give power to enrich our lives.

IDENTIFYING WHAT BELIEFS ARE

Beliefs influence our attitudes, setting general expectations and biases about the world. Believing that a certain race is superior to another can create prejudice. Some beliefs are nebulous and fleeting, others are fixed and tenacious. Some are private and personal, others are shared by whole communities.

EXERCISE 11.1

Establishing what you believe

You are invited to consider your beliefs about the groups and activities listed in the table below. Try using the following formula: 'I believe . . . about . . . because.' Don't spend long on each category. There are no

92

right or wrong answers. When you have worked through them all, go
back over them and try to identify where, and from whom, a particular
belief originated.

What I believe about . . . is . . . because . . .	
Alcoholics	
Arabs	
Asians	
Blacks	
Car salesmen	
Catholics	
Children	
Civil servants	
Clergymen	
Conservatives	
Doctors	
Drug addicts	
Fat people	
Foreigners	
Fox hunting	
French men	
Gun advocates	
Hard-rock music	
Homosexuals	
Intellectuals	
Italians	
Jamaicans	
Jews	
Millionaires	
Motorcycles	
Northerners	
Nurses	
Old people	
Police	
Polish people	
Politicians	
Prostitutes	
Redheads	
Smokers	
Socialists	
Spiders	
The Salvation Army	
Travelling people	
Women	
Women as managers	

Questions

1. Try to determine how you acquired those beliefs.

2. How have those beliefs influenced you?

3. How do those beliefs still influence you?

4. If you had done this exercise ten years ago, how different would your beliefs have been?

5. Are there any beliefs you are hanging on to that no longer serve any useful purpose?

6. Which beliefs would you jettison, and how?

IDENTIFYING WHAT VALUES ARE

As with all aspects of personality, we do not hold one value to the exclusion of all others; but values exert a powerful influence on our lives. Values help to maintain and justify attitudes; the more value-relevant an attitude, the more resistant it is to change. Your values are an important part of your frame of reference, and opposing values are one of the major areas of internal conflict.

An important part of self-counselling is to explore your own values. Many of us take on our parents' (and others') values lock, stock and barrel, but part of developing self-awareness may mean engaging in the painful process of re-evaluating our values and maybe getting rid of some of them; the process of evaluating and getting rid of outworn values never stops.

Identifying six value systems

1. *Political.* The pursuit of power.

2. *Aesthetic.* The pursuit of beauty, symmetry and harmony.

3. *Social.* The pursuit of humanitarianism.

4. *Theoretical.* The pursuit of truth and knowledge.

5. *Economic.* The pursuit of what is utilitarian.

6. *Religious.* The pursuit of faith.

EXERCISE 11.2

Identifying your personal values

This exercise is concerned mainly with personal qualities. Our belief systems and our values are deeply connected. We are motivated and make decisions based on these beliefs and value systems. Often these values are unconscious. We may not know why we choose to lie or stay honest, but we do.

This exercise can be anything you want it to be. You may choose to rank all the values listed; choose a certain number and rank those, or grade them as very important, important, less important. You may also use the words as triggers for a free association or imagery session.

ability to nurture	happiness	reputation
ability to outsmart	honesty	respect from others
acquisitiveness	honour	revenge
affection	independence	security
appearance	integrity	self-realisation
attractiveness	intimacy	self-respect
benevolence	intelligence	service
character	obedience	sex
conventionality	originality	status
creativity	peace	stubbornness
duty	physical fitness	success
excellence	power	talent
family name	privacy	unselfishness
friendship	professionalism	wealth
generosity	religion	youth

Questions

1. Where did you acquire those values?

2. Are any of them now redundant in your life?

3. Are you being driven by someone else's values?

4. Do any of these values force you into unhealthy, stereotyped behaviour? If so, what must you do about it?

EXERCISE 11.3

Assessing your relationship values

In relationships how far do you:

● Assume responsibility for your own feelings, thoughts and actions?

- Show respect by demonstrating that you accept and value the other person?

- Show affection, liking and appreciation? (You can both give and receive.)

- Show commitment to the relationship?

- Show caring and concern for the other person's total well-being?

- Succeed in being open and revealing? (You are trusting and prepared to take risk.)

- Feel safe to give and receive feedback, thereby helping each of you to stay open?

- Avoid being defensive?

- Avoid denying or distorting information in order to remain emotionally comfortable?

- Show understanding through sensitive intuition, knowledge and effective listening?

- Use anger by owning, understanding and handling it constructively?

- Manage conflicts by not turning them into 'I win – you lose' encounters?

- Avoid sexual exploitation, and work for mutual consideration and affection?

- Share activities by allowing the other person time and space?

- Spend time with the other person because your relationship is important to you both?

Questions

1. Which of the above values are essential in your relationship?

2. Which of these values do you need to work on to improve your relationships?

3. Are there any other values you consider important that are not included?

IDENTIFYING STEREOTYPES

One of the ways we cope with differences is to create stereotypes.

Stereotyping is a behaviour that classifies groups of people, generally in unfavourable terms. Stereotyping puts people down, because it attributes to them all the characteristics which we have observed in only a few.

One of the points about stereotyping is that we lump everybody together; this has come to be known as the halo effect – a tendency to allow an overall impression of a person or one particular outstanding trait to influence the total impression of that person. 'All nuns are kind' would be positive statement to demonstrate the halo effect. 'All politicians never speak the truth' would be a negative application. Both are stereotypes, and would not stand up to close scrutiny.

A stereotype has the following characteristics:

● It is a belief about people.

● It is a pattern of behaviour.

● It is relatively fixed.

● It is simplistic.

● It is unjustifiable.

● It allows for no individuality.

● It allows for little or no variation.

● It is often negative.

A very potent application of stereotypes is how we place people in social classes, and attribute certain characteristics to them, simply by their occupations. The idea of social class being linked to occupations is the basis of much of the snobbery in our society. While it may not be so obvious as it was 50 years ago, it is still there.

EXERCISE 11.4

Identifying your social class stereotypes

The discussion now focuses on an exercise in which you can extend your awareness of some of the views, beliefs, values and attitudes towards people from different groups. For each of the occupations listed, create two short statements; one that is discriminatory and one that is accepting and fair. Include how you might behave towards this person. When you have finished, spend some time thinking through why you gave the answers you did.

Identifying your views of others will tell you a lot about your views of yourself. How different would your behaviour be towards a street cleaner than towards a member of the Royal Family?

Actors are	Heads of government are
Administrators are	Labourers are
Anthropologists are	Mail clerks are
Architects are	Managers are
Aristocratic landowners are	Managing Director of the BBC is
Artists are	Mathematicians are
Astronomers are	Merchant bankers are
Bank clerks are	Nursery nurses are
Bank managers are	Nurses are
Biologists are	Office clerks are
Bookkeepers are	Owners of betting shops are
Bus drivers are	Personnel directors are
Car dealers are	Prostitutes are
Civil engineers are	Public school teachers are
Clergy are	Social workers are
Counsellors are	Trade union officials are
Doctors are	Typists are
Drama teachers are	University professors are
Electricians are	University Professors of
Factory workers are	Mathematics are
Garage mechanics are	Word-processor operators are
General practitioners are	Writers are

Checklist

1. Ask yourself why you answered the way you did.

2. Which did you find easiest to make, positive or negative statements?

3. Identify the words that make a statement either positive or negative.

4. Finally, change negatives into a positive and positives into negatives.

5. What did you learn about your values from this exercise?

UNDERSTANDING THE VALUE OF SELF-DETERMINATION

One of the values which most of us cherish is being able to take charge of our own lives, and determine the course our lives will take. Arguments for self-determination are based on the supposition that we are fully responsible for personal actions. It is our basic right of freedom to choose our own direction, even though that decision may clash with the values, beliefs and desires of other people. It also means not choosing to do something we do not feel is right.

Self-determination is not licence. It is influenced by the rights of others; the capacity to make informed decisions; civil and criminal law; and our own morals. When we violate our own moral law, we do spiritual harm to ourselves.

Self-determination cannot be divorced from responsibility to self and to others. But what about suicide? Euthanasia? Abortion? What about pacifism in time of war, and many other moral issues?

One of the functions of counselling is to help clients mobilise their inner resources so that they are more able to make balanced decisions. Many people feel helpless to make decisions because the alternatives are unclear. Helping them tease out what is involved often enables them to make a decision and to take responsibility for what they decide to do. Just so in self-counselling.

Working with the principles of self-determination
In considering self-determination you might find yourself in tension between various rights and duties; between what you want and what other people want; and between two different sets of values. Self-determination can be analysed under the following headings:

1. who is involved and their rights

2. what is involved

3. the possible consequences

4. the possible advantages.

CASE STUDY

Jennifer and Nigel face a dilemma
Jennifer and Nigel married late, and desperately wanted a baby, but Jennifer was 40 years old before she became pregnant. She was advised to have an amniocentesis test, because there was a history of Down's syndrome in her family. The test carried a slight risk of miscarriage. The doctor and their parents were very persuasive, pointing out the greater risk in Jennifer's case, her age, and the fact of having a sister with Down's. Their religious faith would have made a planned abortion unthinkable.

Analysing Jennifer and Nigel's dilemma
Using the four-point structure given above will help to analyse the situation:

1. *Who is involved and their rights.*
   ● Jennifer and Nigel and their respective parents and families.
   ● The rights of the unborn baby.

2. *What is involved.*
   ● The moral and ethical dilemma of interfering with nature.
   ● The question of abortion.
   ● Nine months of uncertainty.

3. *The possible consequences.*
   ● The possibility of an amniocentesis-induced miscarriage.
   ● The possibility of Jennifer not having any more children.
   ● The rights of the wider society, who may have to care for the child if she or he is handicapped, if Jennifer and Nigel cannot continue to care.
   ● The time, energy and cost involved in caring for a handicapped child.
   ● The emotional cost to Jennifer and Nigel of betraying their convictions.

4. *The possible advantages* (of not having the test).
   ● Their religious and moral convictions would not be compromised.
   ● There would be no risk of an amniocentesis-induced miscarriage.

EXERCISE 11.5

Sheila has to make a difficult choice

Sheila had been a nun since the age of 16, over 20years, and had served her Community well in her capacity as a teacher. Over a period of three years she had fallen in love with Jim. Many of her friends reminded her of her vows to God, and put Sheila under a great deal of moral and religious pressure to renounce these desires.

1. Using the four-point structure above and the case study of Jennifer and Nigel, work out how you might help Sheila.

2. How could you use this structure to help you resolve a conflict of values in your own life?

   Turn to the Appendix (page 127) for a suggested answer.

SUMMARY

None of us is value-free. It is important, therefore, that we become aware of the influence our value-judgments exert. Being self-aware weakens our value-judgments so that they are less likely to act as emotional filters, which block the other person's feelings and dictate our responses. Understanding our own values cannot take place in isolation, for just as our values are arrived at as a process of our being exposed to other people, so any change in our value system affects not only ourselves but others also.

Values are an important part of your frame of reference, and being self-aware means that you assume responsibility for your own feelings, thoughts and actions; that you show respect to other people by demonstrating that you accept and value them and their values.

Values are closely linked to judgmentalism, and probably our values are one of the major areas that will bring us into conflict with ourselves and with other people. We must learn that our values are right for us, but we have no right to try to impose them on other people; neither do other people have the right to impose their values on us.

If there is one thing that will get in the way of understanding ourselves or others, of really being in empathy, it is our values. At the same time, it is part of the self-counsellor's task to explore values. In that process, many of the values we have taken on board without thinking (mainly because they were acquired at a young age) come under the self-counselling spotlight. This painful process of re-evaluating our values may mean getting rid of some of them because they are outworn and redundant. That is one of the factors which makes self-counselling so exciting, for we are constantly breaking new ground and moving forward.

12
Working with Thinking and Feelings

STRIVING FOR BALANCE

Several times so far, we have looked at the dimension of thinking/feeling. This chapter will look more deeply at how these two faculties influence our relationships and self-counselling.

Feelings are being conscious of something being agreeable or disagreeable, or, in psychological terms, pleasure or pain. Feelings are an important part of our makeup; an essential part of being alive. Were we not aware of good and evil, of joy and sorrow, of pleasure and pain, we should be no more than a rock on the seashore.

Feelings may arise from something external, through our senses, when we become aware of something happening within us as our bodies respond. Under sensation, we think of feelings arising from the taste of food, the scent of flowers, from light and dark, and from sounds that please or jar.

Feelings also arise from within, from ideas and thoughts. Memory and imagination are two powerful sources of stimulation of feelings. Thinking of something pleasant inevitably brings feelings of satisfaction and pleasure; thinking negative thoughts inevitably brings irritation, even anger and dejection. Human beings like to think, and our ability to do it is usually on the short list of characteristics which distinguish us from other species.

Thinking and feelings are two sides of the coin. As in the discussion on thinking and feeling linked to temperament and preferences in previous chapters, it is essential to strive for a relative balance between these two faculties, for both are related and influence the way we behave.

One of the challenges in life is to keep our feelings well-ordered, so that we don't become ruled by them. At the same time if we hold our feeling on too tight a rein, they will, like the horse who suffers from a bruised mouth, not respond appropriately. If our feelings are constantly subdued by our thinking, they will rebel and instead of thinking and feeling working in harmony, they will be at war.

Identifying the differences between thinking and feeling

- **Thinking (head talk)** is the *prose* of communication. Head talk leads to an explanation of what is going on.

- **Feeling (heart talk)** is the *poetry* of communication. Heart talk leads to an understanding of what is going on.

IDENTIFYING THE THINKING PROCESS

"Think' statements:

- interpret what something means to us

- attempt to define, assert, offer an opinion, rationalise, or make cause and effect connections between different events

- are bound by the rules of logic and scientific inquiry; they may be true or untrue

- can generally be proved or disproved

- require words to be communicated.

Most of us have been trained to make 'I think' statements. We are constantly engaged in observing, inferring, categorising, generalising and summarising. Occasionally we report to others what goes on in our head.

EXERCISE 12.1

Pinpointing confused statements

Many people preface their remarks with 'I feel' and go on to report thoughts. This use of 'I feel' often results in muddled communication. Reconstruct the following three statements as thinking statements:

- **Statement 1**: *I feel like having a drink.*

- **Statement 2**: *I feel that your brashness is a cover for your insecurity.*

- **Statement 3**: *I feel that all men are created equal.*

Turn to the Appendix (page 128) for suggested answers.

IDENTIFYING FEELINGS

'Feel' statements refer to what is implied, internal, immediate, non-rational, emotional; a 'gut' response to something personal and distinctive happening within.

Like dreams, 'feel' statements are neither true or false, good nor bad; they can only be honestly or dishonestly communicated. Many of us have conditioned ourselves to screen out our internal reactions. We allow ourselves to say we feel 'interested', 'uncomfortable', but are scared to disclose our more intense feelings. By getting in touch with what is happening within us, we enrich our own lives and those with whom we communicate.

Changes inside us provide direct clues to the feelings we are experiencing. A change in bodily functioning – muscle tightness, restlessness, frowning, smiling, inability to stay with a conversation – tells us how we are reacting to what is happening.

Identifying blocks to feelings

- *Shame.* Especially when the feeling sounds childish.

- *Fear.* Often associated with not wanting to overstep the mark, or look silly or childish. Fear is often a leftover from the childish thinking.

- *Judgment.* We often expect judgment, yet it can be liberating to express our feelings without shame, fear or judgment.

EXERCISE 12.2

Using imagination with feelings

Stage 1
Try to picture yourself in a situation when you felt:

anger	sadness	joy
fear	embarrassment	guilt
hate	confused	bored
inferior	lonely	rejected

In each situation, try to become aware of what is happening in your mind, body and your emotions. When you are aware of something happening in your body, mind or emotions, try to stay with it and not shrug it off. The more you allow your feelings to speak to you, the more self-understanding you will gain and the more accurate will be your understanding of your own and other people's feelings.

Stage 2
Take one of the words you worked with, perhaps one that caused you the most pain or discomfort. Write an imaginary letter to a close friend. Make it a factual one, without any feelings in it.

Rewrite your letter, and for every fact you identify, include one or more feelings you associate with the fact. Assess the difference between the two letters.

OWNING YOUR THOUGHTS AND FEELINGS

Effective self-communication (and communication with others) occurs when we take responsibility for our thoughts, feelings and behaviour, when we own what we do. Blaming, attributing motives, claiming that 'the devil made me do it' are sneaky, dishonest attempts to be irresponsible. When we own our thoughts and feelings, we (and other people) know where we are and can respond more authentically.

We are entitled to our thoughts and feelings. Being aware of them, and the differences between them, is one way to improve self-awareness.

EXERCISE 12.3

Saying what you feel

1. List a number of different situations in which you project, blame or imply motives.

2. Make a list of 'think statements' which masquerade as 'feel statements'.

3. Write a number of sentences beginning with 'Right now I'm aware of . . .' or sentences ending with '. . . and I take responsibility for it.'

UNDERSTANDING THE ADVANTAGES OF EXPRESSING FEELINGS

You have the right to express your positive and negative feelings, though this has to be done in a way that does not damage other people, for they also have rights.

- We should neither discourage nor condemn feelings.

- Expressing feelings relieves pressure and tension and frees us for positive, constructive action.

- Expressing feelings helps us to understand our difficulties more clearly.

- Expressing feelings helps us assess our strengths and weaknesses.

- When feelings are brought into the open, there is more chance that we can do something constructive with them.

- Feelings are as real as facts. Let feelings speak for themselves! Let us ensure that we listen to them.

- When we deny our feelings, fears, hopes and hostilities, we do not deal with ourselves as whole people.

EXERCISE 12.4

Being honest about your feelings

Before you can explore feelings you must be aware of them. Then you can own them as yours. In each of these questions try to be open with yourself.

1.   The feeling I find easiest to express is:

2.   The feeling I find most difficult to express is:

3.   The person I feel most at ease with is:

4.   The person I feel most uncomfortable with is:

5.   The thing I find easiest to do is:

6.   The thing I find most difficult to do is:

7.   The one thing about myself I would most wish to alter is:

Challenge yourself

1. Do you want to own these feelings?

2. Would you be prepared for someone else to know this about you?

3. Why would you not want to disclose these feelings with anyone?

EXERCISE 12.5

Recognising feelings

Feelings are our reactions to our inner world and the world around us. We all vary in our ability to express our feelings. Some of us are able to identify every nuance of feelings; others find it a struggle to even identify such basic feelings as mad, glad, sad and afraid. To be effective self-counsellors we need to develop a wide vocabulary of feeling words.

Your task

Find as many words as you can that will fit into the categories – Anger, Joy, Grief and Fear. Turn to the Appendix (page 128) for suggested answers.

EXERCISE 12.6

Expanding your feelings vocabulary

Use the diagram in Figure 12. For this exercise a good dictionary or a thesaurus is helpful.

1. Fill the second square with words that express love. Select one word from the second square.

2. Fill the third square with words that express your chosen word. Select one word from the third square.

3. Fill the fourth square with words that express your chosen word. Select one word from the fourth square.

4. Fill the fifth square with words that express your chosen word.

How many words have you found linked to the word love?

If you feel inclined, take any other word in any of your four squares and repeat the exercise. At whichever stage you decide to stop, you will have added many, many words to your feelings vocabulary. This exercise can be adapted to any other word or groups of words.

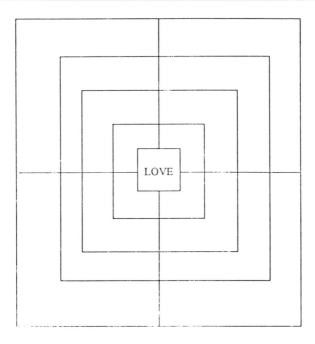

Fig. 12. The feelings square.

EXERCISE 12.7

Vocabulary test

Finding words that express similar or near meanings is an important skill in self-counselling. Improving your vocabulary is one way of developing your self-awareness. Your task in the list below is to find one word which stands for the four synonyms in each line.

When you have finished all 20 questions, turn to the Appendix (page 129) where you will find the correct answers.

Synonyms	Your word
1. agitate, disturb, impinge upon, penetrate	....
2. admire, cherish, esteem, treasure	....
3. altruism, charity, generosity, munificence	....
4. abreaction, cleansing, purging, purifying	....
5. ardent, eager, resolute, zealous	....
6. hysterical, uncontrolled, tear-jerking, heated	....
7. avid, devoted, keen, spirited	....
8. changeable, erratic, mercurial, volatile	....
9. animate, arouse, enthuse, motivate	....

10. ability, faculty, knack, tendency   ....
11. discernment, gut feeling, insight, presentiment   ....
12. amorous, vehement, hot-tempered, torrid   ....
13. feeble, inadequate, miserable, woebegone   ....
14. dedicated, goody-goody, moralistic, saintly   ....
15. antipathy, bias, intolerance, narrow-mindedness   ....
16. animosity, bitterness, irritation, umbrage   ....
17. artificial, emotionalism, mawkish, slush   ....
18. candour, frankness, probity, genuineness   ....
19. cloistered, remoteness, seclusion, retirement   ....
20. commiseration, condolence, pity, fellow-feeling   ....

CASE STUDY

James needs help to reflect feelings

James related a dream. 'I'm sitting at a desk in a library. Behind me I know there's a frightening figure, dressed in academic gown, pointing a cane at me. The book on the desk is huge. As I turn the pages, the words disappear, like they've been hit by a computer virus. Panic hits me in the stomach. How can I ever get to grips with this if the words disappear? I slam the book shut, saying "I'll never pass." Printed on the front cover in large, gold letters is one word, "James". I wake up, feeling exhausted.'

A few days before this, James had been in a counselling workshop. My colleague, Anne, who was working with James, said to him, in the plenary session, 'You have a fine brain, and you analyse the client's statement very well, and your interpretations are spot on. However, you have difficulty reflecting the client's feelings. My hunch is that this is because you have difficulty identifying and sharing your own feelings. This is something for you to work on.'

EXERCISE 12.8

Interpreting James's dream

You are invited to interpret James's dream. Turn to the Appendix (page 130) for his interpretation.

SUMMARY

Thinking and feeling are essential elements of being alive, and one is the flip side of the other. Thoughts have the habit of flitting in and out of our consciousness at amazing speed. They can linger or they can become so lodged in our minds that they pester. They can be like the will-o'-the-wisp, leading us a merry dance into dangerous areas. They can be silent like the grave or as noisy as a busload of children on the way to school.

Thoughts are such changeable things and yet they can be so persistent as to exert a powerful influence on our behaviour. They can lift us to lofty heights or plunge us into the depths of despair and degradation. So in our quest for self-awareness we need to get in touch with our thought life and how our behaviour is influenced by it.

Feelings may be identified as being surface and implied. As you continue with self-counselling, you will find that you move increasingly from working with surface (not unimportant) feelings to deeper ones, as you gain more confidence and self-awareness. It is as if your psyche has been preparing the way, laying foundations for your exploration.

Exploration of feelings requires that you understand them and this is a thinking process. The more balanced your thinking and feeling functions, the deeper your self-awareness. The deeper your self-awareness, the further you will be able to travel along that particular road.

13
Working with your Life Story

This chapter is based on the work of Charles V. Gerkin, professor of pastoral psychology at Emory University, who draws upon the work of another visionary, Anton Boisen. Although Gerkin was writing about pastoral counselling, many of the concepts apply to self-counselling.

In his book, *The Living Human Document*, Gerkin sees people in crisis as being caught between despair on the one hand, and an interpretation of hope and expectation on the other. Much of the problem of the crisis experience is seen as a loss of the sense of continuity, coupled with a loss of hope and faith.

LISTENING TO YOUR OWN STORY

While any counsellor listens to and interprets other people's stories, in substance this is no different from self-counselling as you struggle through the pain of tangled emotions and experiences. During self-counselling, you listen to yourself and try to make sense of what, at times, seems senseless. In this chapter, you counsel yourself to change the plot of your life story.

Unlike counselling, self-counselling does not depend upon someone else to identify, reflect and explore themes and feelings; to engage with your frame of reference. The language of the counsellor might not match yours. The meaning you attribute to experiences, the symbols and images used may not match the counsellor's. It is as if you and another person have a dividing boundary between you.

While this boundary does not exist in self-counselling, what the self-counsellor does miss is the mind of another person. Your exploration is limited by self-awareness and the willingness to go where you might never have gone before. Even though your psyche is an accurate and ever-present guide, hearing something through another person's frame of reference can be challenging and rewarding. It is incumbent upon the counsellor to strive to understand the client's language, symbols, concepts and images, the personal meanings. Failure to do this will result in fatal stereotyping and the client will leave empty-handed.

Bearing in mind that as self-counsellor you will have to strive to be objective and be able to perform a balancing act between being yourself and, as it were, someone else, there is no reason why your journey of self-awareness should not continue to be rewarding.

WORKING WITH YOURSELF AS AN OPEN BOOK

Anton Boisen, generally considered the founder of clinical pastoral education in America, coined the term 'living human documents' to highlight how essential it is that there is no better way to experience people than to listen to them; to read and interpret them as 'living human documents'.

Understanding and interpreting your own story will give you insight into your inner world. Just as the text of, say, Dickens' *The Pickwick Papers* and Shakespeare's *Midsummer Night's Dream* are different, so is your life story different from that of anyone else. This relates to the unique self, discussed in Chapter 10.

People who come for counselling are usually aware of the suffering that comes from being stuck in their past, although that awareness may be hazy. Self-counselling aims to liberate your inner resources and, if you feel you are suffering, to enable you to handle the suffering more positively and help to restore your identity which suffering has damaged.

EXERCISE 13.1

Tracking your story

It is a curious fact, but many of us do not take sufficient time to ask many of the important questions about who we are, where we have come from or where we would like to be going. The more we know about what influences us, the more control we will be able to exert on our life. These 15 questions tie in with Exercise 3.2 – Using your Life Chart to develop your self-awareness, in Chapter 3.

1. What is the first experience that you can remember?
   What feelings do you have about this experience?

2. What were your favourite stories when you were a child?
   Who were your favourite fictional heroes and heroines?

3. When you were a child, were you co-operative, competitive, fearful, negative?
   What were your best and worst subjects at school?
   Which subjects did you like and dislike?

4. What do you remember about your childhood patterns of eating and exercising?

5. How did you make friends in primary school, then later?

6. When you were a child, whom did you want to imitate?

7. What qualities did you particularly admire?

8. How did you feel towards relatives other than your parents?

9. How would you describe the general atmosphere of your home life?

10. What was the attitude of each of your parents towards you?

11. What was your attitude towards your parents?

12. What moral and/or religious instruction did you receive in your home?

13. What special enjoyments of your early home life do you most treasure?

14. What events, accompanied by great happiness, success, joy, have shaped your life?

15. What events involving great sadness, discomfort, fear, humiliation, failure, transgression have shaped your life?

Your overall story

Briefly review your responses and any notes that you have made. In a few paragraphs, summarise your story so far, the changes you would like to make and how you plan to set about making those changes.

Keep in mind that you are a product of what you inherited and past experiences, all of which influence you as you are now. By examining yourself and your environment calmly and thoroughly, you can achieve a grasp of your alternatives and take action to create the life that you want.

Identifying three life forces in your story

The task of the psyche is to hold in tension the three life forces of Ego, Society and Beliefs. The constant interaction between all three life forces makes up the flow of life in which the self is nurtured, or kept in bondage.

The ego is your perception of who you are; the part that is in touch with reality, and influenced by the external world and dealing with external and internal stimulation. Ego tensions arise from conflicts that emerge in the course of psychological development.

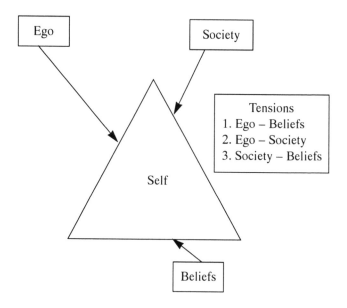

Fig. 13. Identifying three life forces in your story.

Society tensions arise from:

- economic constraints, cultural, class, race

- immediate community, work, family

- relationships

- expectations, commitments, conformity.

Beliefs tensions arise from:

- faith, myths and symbols of a culture shaped over time

- language, by which behaviours and relationships are given meanings and the way an individual perceives self and the world

- culture, which tells us which thoughts and behaviour should be assigned guilty, accusatory meaning and which should receive commendation.

EXERCISE 13.2

Working with the life force model

Think of your life as the triangle: Ego, Society, Beliefs (see Figure 13). Using the three boxes in Figure 14, ask yourself: What questions could I ask that would help me to understand myself from each of these three standpoints?

Ego

- What do you think and feel about yourself?
- What is your level of self-esteem?
- How do you relate to yourself?
- How comfortable are you with yourself and with others?
- What are your relationships like?
- What are your strengths and weaknesses?
- Any other questions and answers?

Society

- How do you relate to society and what do you think of your place in society?
- What are your relationships with various significant sections of society: parents, siblings, friends?
- What are your views about work?
- How would you describe your fit with society, or are you uncomfortable in it?
- Do you feel more at ease with certain groups in society than with others? If so, why?
- Any other questions and answers.

Beliefs

- What are your beliefs about life and death?
- What are your views about different faiths and religions?
- What are the foundations of your beliefs?
- How do your beliefs relate to Ego and Society?
- How do myths and symbols influence you?
- What are your beliefs about right and wrong, about crime and punishment?
- How do your values influence what you believe?
- Any other questions and answers?

Fig. 14. Ego, Society and Beliefs.

Identifying tensions

When you have all your statements you can start to piece them together. From each of the three boxes, take one thing at a time and contrast and compare it with those from the others. In this way you start to get some idea of the tensions that exist between them.

In order for a triangle to retain its shape, each of the sides must be in balance, and when there is undue pressure on one side of the triangle, the whole will collapse. So if you think of the tensions as pressure trying to distort the triangle you might have a better understanding of the model.

IDENTIFYING CHAPTERS IN YOUR OWN BOOK

Working with yourself as a book, consciously or unconsciously, you dip into different 'chapters' in your life story. You may have been conscious of this many times as you have worked through the various exercises in this book, and in Exercise 13.1 above.

For every stage in life, every significant event, every relationship of meaning, every joy, sorrow, pain or pleasure, there is a chapter. Sometimes there are chapters that remain open, long after we think they were closed. Unclosed chapters cause us pain, as we can't move forward while they are still open, as if they keep saying. 'Hi! I'm still here, and I can't be put to rest.' Healing can only take place as we find the courage to open the book, and work through the unclosed chapter.

Joan came for counselling because of a deep grief following the death of her beloved cat. Exploration of the life story revealed an unclosed chapter – the death of her older sister, when Joan was only two years old, and too young to consciously 'remember'.

In my own case, ten years after my father's death I knew I had to go into that particular chapter and work with the pain, anger and loss, and close the chapter. Yet out of the pain did come healing, and so it can be for you.

EXERCISE 13.3

Dipping into your own book

Taking any of the points of Exercise 13.1, imagine each of these as a chapter of your book.

1. Give the book a title, with chapter headings.

2. Scan the book for any unclosed chapters, and let your psyche guide you into which chapter to work on.

3. Identify the facts and the feelings associated with that event or period in your life.

4. Use imagery to resolve any conflicts or to bring healing.

Before leaving this exercise, try to close at least one chapter. Take time to adjust to reality before you pick up the threads of the present.

CASE STUDY

Rex is not being honest

Rex, a minister, 45 years of age, married to Rosemary, with three children, was stressed, unable to sleep, lacked concentration, had a poor appetite. Sexual relationships were strained. His preaching, he felt, lacked power and authority. His expressed fear was that he was losing his grip. Over the past few years they had seen the church congregation double numerically and there had been great spiritual growth. At the same time, he and Rosemary were seeing less of each other, because of the demands which the church made on both of them.

Over several sessions, he and Peter, another minister, established a healthy relationship, where Rex felt safe. In session three he said, 'It's no good, Peter, I haven't been honest with you. There's another woman. I haven't been faithful to my vows to Rosemary.' Peter slowly learned that over several months Rex had become involved with Anita, one of the women who was active in the fellowship, also married with children. 'I feel caught in a vicious trap,' Rex said, struggling to keep his tears from spilling over. 'I've been living a lie for so long. Rosemary suspects, but doesn't know. I don't know if she's told the children. I can't think what it will do to them, or me, or Anita and her family. I feel like ending it all, I honestly do. How can I face my congregation now?'

EXERCISE 13.4

Creating a response to Rex

The feelings which Peter identified were: anxiety, betrayed, dejected, disgrace, distressed, doubts, failure, fearful, lost, miserable, pain, powerless, responsibility, slipping, sorrow, tapped, troubled, two-timing, uncertainty.

How would you continue with Rex? Using the model of Ego, Society and Beliefs, create a response. When you have done this, turn to the Appendix (page 130) and compare your response with the one given.

Creating a response, *as if you were addressing someone else*, is a super way of learning to relate to yourself.

SUMMARY

The end of this book seemed a natural place to put this chapter – working with your life story – for all the way through the previous chapters there has been some exploration of that story.

Some people might question the advisability of trying to explore your own 'living document', to use Anton Boisen's term, but it could be equally argued – who better than yourself, if you've taken on board what has been written so far: taking things gently, not pushing for insights too deep or too fast, trusting your psyche to guide you – then you have acquired many skills and insights to help you make sense of your own story.

Having someone to whom you can turn, a mentor, when you feel stuck is certainly a boon, and such a relationship will not only provide support but also add to your self-awareness. Counsellors who are working through this book will invariably have their own supervision support system, and both you and your supervisor could benefit from approaching your clients' life stories from another angle.

As you work through your story you may find it painful and difficult to narrate, even to yourself. What you explore may not be *the* story, but merely a connecting line. Many side avenues need to be explored before the central story emerges clearly. If you experience some sense of an obstruction, damming of the flow, you may need to rest for a while and wait for your psyche to guide you.

Using imagery is one way of identifying what the blockage is. Using the word 'blockage' as a trigger, try to find an image that represents that blockage, then create a non-harmful way of removing the blockage. Above all, trust your psyche to guide you. I hope you will find the courage and strength to close at least one previously unclosed chapter.

FINALE

This book has been a mix of theory and practice, and I hope that you feel comfortable with being your own counsellor. In every chapter the aim has been to engage you in all that is taking place. Just how far I have succeeded in doing that I may never know, but if you have added some insights, and learned some skills in becoming your own counsellor, then there has been some engagement or involvement.

Engaging someone is like driving a car. For the car to move, the gears have to be engaged. Just so in this process of self-counselling. In counselling between two people, if there is no involvement, there will be no movement. There has to be a meeting of minds and spirits of the two people, and together they move forward.

In self-counselling there is only you, and yet by now you may be aware that you are not alone; that there is someone 'riding tandem'. You may have found it uncomfortable to work with the idea of the psyche, yet having such an intimate travelling companion can be an experience beyond mere words.

Learning to listen to yourself, to become aware of the inner workings of your body, mind and spirit, all within the safety of your own chosen space, can be liberating and exhilarating. If you have felt comfortable with having your psyche as your confidant and guide, then you have made friends with a vital part of yourself.

As you end this book, try to apply the skills and insights to your life. And having reached the last words, may you continue to move forward and apply the insights and skills to any situation in life where you feel the need to engage your travelling companion, who will go with you towards whichever goal you decide upon.

Appendix:
Resources and Solutions
for Exercises

EXERCISE 1.1

Here is my imaginary solution.

Thinking. I can't go down or around. And I don't want to go back. The landslide looks too dangerous to climb over, and I might kill myself. As this is pure imagination, I can do whatever I want. I look around for inspiration. Hanging from a small tree I discover a pair of boots. They don't look to be anything out of the ordinary, but I know they are there for a reason. I fasten them on, and feel energised, so much so that I start jumping up and down. Suddenly I'm soaring over the obstacle powered by these magic boots.

EXERCISE 2.2

Themes as triggers for free association

abandoned	blind	direction
adolescence	blockage	disappointments
adulthood	bored	disapproval
aggression	brother(s)	discouragement
air	career	doctor
anger	children	dominant
anniversary	clothes	door
anxiety	country	earth
appearance	creative	education
apprehension	crossroads	embarrassment
approval	deaf	embrace
attraction	death	eternity
ball	defences	evasive
benevolence	dentist	excellence
birth	depression	expectations
birthday	deserted	face
blame	desires	failures

fantasy
father
fear
feelings
feet
feminist
fire
flowers
fool
friends
friendship
garden
genitals
giving
goals
gossip
grandparent
grass
grief
guilt
hair
hands
happiness
hate
health
heaven
hell
homosexual
hospital
house
hurt
independence
inhibition
influence
innocence
integration
integrity
irritation
leisure
limbo
locality
love

manipulation
martyr
mask
mirror
money
moon
mother
neurotic
nurse
nursery
obstacle
offence
opportunities
optimism
outsider
pain
panic
parents
passive
partner
pessimism
pilgrim
planets
play
power
prayer
prison
progress
psychiatrist
punishment
rational
rebel
receiving
redundant
regrets
rejection
relationships
religious
resistance
retirement
river
road

rules
school
sea
secrets
self-esteem
sexual
shadow
shame
sister(s)
sorrow
spendthrift
sports
spouse
stairs
stars
strangers
strategies
stream
strength
stress
stupid
successes
suffering
sun
teachers
thoughts
timidity
touch
town
trap
trauma
water
weakness
wholeness
window
wisdom
work
worry
worship

EXERCISE 3.2

Your Life Chart

Period of life	Event	Thoughts, feelings, behaviours
Year 1	Birth plus	
Year 2		
Year 3		
And so on		

EXERCISE 4.3

Interpreting James's dream (outline)

1. *Antecedents*: James had been doing work on the relationship with his father.

2. *Atmosphere*: sun, clouded over.

3. *Feelings, expressed*: frustration.

4. *Feelings, implied*: happy, contented.

5. *People*: father. Possibility of lock-keeper.

6. *Symbols*: boats, sun, water, stream, lock, canal, direction, helm, father.

7. *Conflicts*: direction, taking over.

8. *Links with previous dreams*: none identified.

Expansion

1. *Antecedents*. The fact that James had been doing work on the rela-

tionship with his father indicated that he was 'ready' for the next stage.

2. *Atmosphere.* The whole scene speaks of contentment, happiness. Clouds indicate something passing in front of the sun, obscuring, creating less warmth, a feeling of coldness.

5. *People.* The father is the most significant other person. The lock-keeper is implied. He is the one who would control the gates. The one who has control. Yet he remains a shadowy figure. It seems that the control is switched to the father.

6. *Symbols*:
   - *Boat.* A boat or ship implies a journey, and a journey consists of navigating to reach the desired goal. As in all symbolism, it is necessary to explore the purpose of the particular object being considered. Expanding the image in this way keeps adding to the symbolism.
   - *Sun.* The sun gives light and warmth; it separates night from day; it is the giver of life; it marks the seasons. The sun shows us the way, and is something that is constant.
   - *Water.* Water is one of the four primal elements – fire, water, air and earth. Water is symbolic of the unconscious, and intuition.
   - *Rivers and streams* are similar in symbolism, except that the stream is usually faster flowing, and not so deep as the river. Both have origins and destinations, though streams end up in rivers, or lakes, while rivers end up in seas, sometimes in dams, often in oceans. River is an analogy of the journey down the river of life.
   - *Lock.* A canal lock is symbolic of control, of waiting. It also represents height and depth, as the water rises. It represents being trapped, for when the boat is in the lock, there is no way out.
   - *Canal.* Like a stream or river, the association is with water. But a canal is different from both stream and river, in that it is man-made, for the specific purpose of transporting goods from one point to another. Thus a canal links the sea with somewhere else. It is a connection. It could also represent the journey of life. It could also represent the birth process.
   - *Direction.* Water flows in one direction, downhill. The two main associations of direction are backward and forward.
   - *Helm.* This symbolises taking control, guiding the boat.
   - *Father.* I have included 'father' here because it is a strongly

archetypal figure, invested with authority, power. The father-image stands for the past and the present, for moral commandments, prohibitions and control of the instincts; the son-image stands for the future, and for liberty.

One possible interpretation

James said, 'This dream spoke very powerfully to me of where I thought I was, not at all certain if I, or my father, or someone else, was in charge of my life. The fact that I decided to travel upstream spoke to me of my determination.' We then spent time opening up the dream, as follows.

1. James took encouragement from my suggestion that he was now ready to look more closely at the relationship with his father. The fact that his father appeared at a time when he was feeling frustrated and stuck seemed important. Was this James saying that he still needed him, and would like to have him alongside? They were travelling together, and his father 'lent a hand'. James was OK about that. It is also possible that although James was 'steering his own boat', he also needed help.

2. James, himself, interpreted the determination. There is the fact that the boat was going forward, away from the sea. This is symbolic of travelling towards the origin of things, to the source.

3. The sun: was this a play on words – son and sun? If it was so (and I have often found myself laughing in my dream at such word games!), and as the 'sun' was obscured by clouds, was the 'son' obscured by the father?

4. Lock: the fact that James was impatient in the lock could indicate his impatience with the process. He could feel trapped, and it would have been interesting to get James to feel himself back into the lock; to become the lock. But just as the water in the lock cannot be hurried, so the psyche will not be hurried.

5. As in 2, James was travelling along something that linked two different things. As it turned out, he interpreted this as his past and future. His father made a short appearance (in the present) then left. This could have been the psyche telling James that he was now in control; master of his own ship.

6. The helm, or tiller, of a boat is what gives it guidance, direction and safety. A broken tiller spells disaster. The fact that the father took the helm at one stage could indicate that James's internal father, the

adult, the authority figure within him, was assuming control. And this ties in with James's words, 'but I still wasn't sure if I was in charge.' Who is in charge of his life? Himself, or his father?

EXERCISE 5.1

Trigger words for imagery

accolade	dawn	hammer
alarm	decoy	harmony
ambush	desert	harp
ancestor	devil	harvest
annihilate	dilemma	hatchet
battleaxe	double bind	haven
beggar	duel	hero/heroine
blemish	eclipse	holocaust
blind spot	effigy	homage
bondage	emblem	homosexual
boycott	enclosure	horizon
brainwash	envelop	hostage
bridge	erase	hug
bulwark	euthanasia	humble
burden	excommunicate	hurricane
cage	exile	impulsive
captive	exterminate	incest
castaway	facade	individuality
Catch-22	famine	infantile
chain gang	fanfare	inferior
chrysalis	fetter	inheritance
cloister	feud	innocence
cloud nine	flotsam	interrogation
confined	forbidden fruit	intimacy
conquest	fortress	invasion
cord	fugitive	investigation
coward	funeral	judge
cradle	guardian angel	killing
crown	guide	labyrinth
culprit	gulf	liberty
curfew	gutter	limbo
curse	halo	mad
dagger	halter	manacle

marathon	pledge	seclusion
martyr	poverty	servant
massacre	predator	shrine
mentor	prestige	shroud
mire	pride	slavery
miser	privacy	stigma
mourning	pry	straitjacket
nightmare	puncture	strangle
nuisance	punishment	suffocate
numb	puppet	suicide
oasis	quarrel	talisman
obstruction	racism	tornado
opponent	rage	traitor
oppression	ransack	trappings
origin	ransom	truant
orphan	rape	tunnel
overture	refuge	union
pagan	remnant	vespers
parable	restraint	vice
pauper	revolt	voyage
pawn	rubbish	weapon
peacemaker	ruthless	wilderness
peak	sacrifice	yoke
phoenix	sanctuary	zealot
pioneer	scapegoat	zest
plateau	scourge	

EXERCISE 5.2

Images
Flat, mountain, plateau, valley, river, rest, mountain top, brightness, determination, companion, time.

Possible interpretation

- *Flat* is a word to express a mood of being low, depressed, fed up. Associated words are pushed down, dejection, despair, gloom, downhearted, sadness, melancholy, discouragement, despondency, gloominess, glumness, the blues, unhappiness.

- *Mountain.* This has to be considered in relation to the surrounding landscape. Generally it represents difficulties to be overcome, exploration, the conquest of aspirations. Mountains are associated with valleys. The mountain top obscured by mist or clouds suggests mystery, everything not yet revealed. To reach the top requires effort and determination.

- *Plateau.* A plateau is a place to rest, and catch one's breath, to look backward and upward.

- *Valley.* A valley is a fertile place, as distinct from the mountain.

- *River.* See the discussion earlier in this Appendix, Exercise 4.3, interpreting James's dream.

- *Rest.* The meaning here seems obvious. We need to rest after exertion. Climbing as far as the plateau means effort.

- *Brightness.* This means expectation, often in contrast with dull, sombre, dark. It can also mean hope in contrast with despair; the future in contrast with the past. Brightness draws one forward.

- *Determination.* A symbolic feeling which contrasts with wavering. So the plateau was a place of decision, to go back or go on.

- *Companion.* Many people long for companionship, particularly when engaged in struggle. Susan wanted to be on her own. Something she needed to do for and by herself? A companion often appears in imagery, frequently in the form of a 'wise' person, a guide, a mentor. This is the psyche's way of ensuring you are not alone.

- *Time.* Susan points to a vital point about imagery. The deeper one is involved, the longer it often takes to re-enter the 'real' world. The return journey should never be hurried.

EXERCISE 11.5

1. *Who is involved and their rights.*
   - Sheila and Jim.
   - The Community, and the college she served.

2. *What is involved.*
   - Sheila's vows of life-long service to the Church.
   - Reconciling her wish with her faith.

3. *The possible consequences.*
   - Living in a sexual relationship.
   - Living away from the Community.

- Not being understood by other people.
- Being considered 'selfish'.

4. *The possible advantages.*
   - Their love would be fulfilled.
   - They would have much to give to a new community.

EXERCISE 12.1

Statement 1 – Rephrased: *I'm thinking about having a drink, but I'm still undecided.*

Statmenet 2 – Rephrased: *It's my opinion that you cover up your insecurity with brashness.*

Statement 3 – Rephrased. *I believe that all men are created equal.*

EXERCISE 12.5

Words associated with anger

Aggravated	Displeased	Hostile	Provoked
Angry	Enmity	Incensed	Rage
Animosity	Enraged	Indignant	Rancour
Antagonistic	Exasperated	Inflamed	Revenge
Bitter	Fret	Infuriated	Sore
Boiling	Frustrated	Irked	Steamed-up
Bothered	Fuming	Miffed	Vexed
Detestable	Furious	Passion	Worked-up
Disgusted	Hateful	Peeved	Wrath

Words associated with joy

Alive	Ecstatic	Hilarious	Pleasure
Blessed	Elated	Jolly	Proud
Blithe	Enchanted	Jovial	Rapturous
Calm	Energetic	Jubilant	Satisfied
Cheery	Enjoyment	Light-hearted	Serene
Comfortable	Excited	Merry	Spirited
Complacent	Exuberant	Overjoyed	Tranquil
Content	Glee	Peace	Vibrant
Delighted	Grateful	Placid	Warm
Ease	Happy	Pleased	Zest

Words associated with grief

Agony	Disappointed	Hopeless	Resigned
Anguish	Disconsolate	Humbled	Remorse
Ashamed	Discouraged	Humiliated	Sadness
Beaten	Dismal	Hurt	Shame
Bleak	Dispirited	Let down	Solemn
Blue	Distant	Lonely	Sombre
Bored	Down	Melancholy	Sorrow
Bruised	Downcast	Miserable	Sullen
Cheerless	Embarrassed	Morose	Turned off
Crestfallen	Empty	Mournful	Unfulfilled
Defeated	Forlorn	Moved	Unhappy
Deflated	Gloomy	Numb	Uninterested
Dejected	Grieving	Pained	Unsettled
Despair	Grim	Pessimistic	Unworthy
Despondent	Heavy	Regret	Woe
Devastated	Helpless	Rejected	Worthless

Words associated with fear

Agitated	Doubtful	Jittery	Tense
Alarmed	Dubious	Lost	Terrified
Alone	Edgy	Nervous	Threatened
Anxious	Fainthearted	Panic	Timid
Apprehensive	Fearful	Perturbed	Timorous
Cautious	Fidgety	Petrified	Tremulous
Concerned	Frightened	Reluctant	Troubled
Cowardly	Ghastly	Restless	Unconfident
Coy	Hesitant	Scared	Uneasy
Diffident	Inadequate	Sceptical	Unsure
Disinclined	Inferior	Shaky	Uptight
Disoriented	Insecure	Shocked	Vulnerable
Distressed	Intimidated	Started	Worried

EXERCISE 12.7

1. Affect	6. Emotional	11. Intuition	16. Resentment
2. Appreciate	7. Enthusiastic	12. Passionate	17. Sentimental
3. Benevolence	8. Fickle	13. Pathetic	18. Sincerity
4. Cathartic	9. Inspire	14. Pious	19. Solitude
5. Earnest	10. Instinct	15. Prejudice	20. Sympathy

EXERCISE 12.8

James was being 'driven' by the schoolmaster figure behind him to make sense of something that kept disappearing before his eyes; something he couldn't grasp hold of – his feelings. The schoolmaster figure could have been a re-creation of Anne, who had challenged him, and by so doing had given him work to do. The fact that he was reading a book suggests that he thought he could get what he needed from the library – head knowledge. But the disappearing words suggest that the book was not the answer. At the same time, but not until in frustration he shut the book did he realise it, he *was* the book. The answer lay not in the printed word but in discovering more about himself.

EXERCISE 13.4

Working with the feelings he identified, Peter said 'Rex, you are feeling a lot of pain and visible distress and conflict about where you are right now. There is a great deal of fear about your present situation; how you are going to face Rosemary and your family, Anita and her family, and your congregation. I hear the disgrace in your voice of having betrayed your vows to God and to Rosemary, as well as to the community of faith. You feel trapped in a relationship which is ungodly, and therefore, for you, unhealthy. It seems that you have lived a lie for so long that you're not sure if you can redeem yourself, and perhaps you are terrified of rejection by the people who have been hurt. In fact, it all seems so awful and black that you see suicide as a possible way out of the trap you feel yourself to be in.'

Beliefs

'Rex, it seems that there are three areas which we could profitably look at, to try to help you sort out your feelings and to get some sort of action. The first is your relationship to God. You are a man of the community, appointed by God to be a shepherd of the flock. The vows you made are in conflict with your behaviour and with the moral code your preaching has made public.'

Society

'The second area is your relationship with society. Firstly, there is the community of faith – your congregation, particularly Anita and her family, and your own family. Secondly, there is the wider community of faith, of which, as a clergyman, you are a significant part. Towards Anita and her family I sense a feeling of having betrayed their trust. The relationship with your wife and family has been put under enormous strain, a strain that has probably been hidden, but nonetheless there, for as long as the affair has been going on.

'The relationship with your congregation has been violated and this can only bring severe pain to everyone concerned. From what you have said, I know you believe that when one member of the body hurts, all members experience something of that hurt. At the moment, although you have not made the affair public, your congregation, in some way, is also caught up in your struggle, without being consciously aware of the reasons. While this may be true for your family and the congregation, the pain and anguish will increase when the situation is disclosed. Then the wider community of faith, and society in general, will be caught up in blame and recrimination, and your pain will be intensified.'

Ego

'The third area is your view of yourself. As a minister, I guess you have a view of yourself as a responsible and reliable person, honest and trust-worthy. Also as a minister, you care for people. Your church has grown over the past few years, and we have all appreciated working with you in this growth process. Right now, however, I see a man who is broken, betrayed by himself, very uncertain as to who he is, and not at all sure what the future holds. Apart from me and Anita, nobody else knows, though some may suspect. One of the struggles you have is: do you break off this relationship and tell no one, or brave the storm and con-fess? What to do and just how to do it is putting you into monumental conflict.'

Tensions

'The last area to look at are the tensions between these three areas. It seems to me that your view of God now doesn't quite tally with the view you had before you became entangled in a relationship which, in your words, was not of God's making. Although I am making a few assump-tions here, I think you believed that we worship a loving and forgiving God. Yet you talk about 'ending it all'. That is in conflict with what you truly believe, I am certain. If God can forgive our sins, any of them, he can and will forgive you, if you truly repent. Ending it all, as you sug-gest, would be but a further betrayal of all you believe.

'Your family and congregation will be in turmoil, and some will revile you. They may well feel that they can no longer trust you, and this will cause great conflict with your view of yourself, as a loving husband and father and a pastor. I'm not suggesting you regard yourself as an idol, but when people discover that their idol has feet of clay, the reve-lation may seem too much for you to bear.

'Overall, Rex, your private and public view of God, with all the beliefs surrounding that, is under severe strain as a result of events. God will not cast you off, like an unwanted work rag, any more than you would have done with one of your flock before all this happened. Your family and congregation will be stunned at the news; those who truly love you will help you pull through. Those who do not love you will say harsh things and many will judge you and this will affect your numbers. In the end, Rex, your decision, as I see it, is: Can I trust God and those I love? Do I trust myself, to do what, in my heart, I feel I must do, for God's sake, the sake of the community of faith and for my own peace of mind?'

Note: This is a very long response, and you may need to read it several times to get hold of all the issues.

Glossary

Affect. A subjective emotion or feeling attached to an idea, to some aspect of self, or to some object. Common affects are euphoria, anger and sadness. Affect may be flat, blunted, inappropriate, labile.

Amniocentesis test. A procedure for withdrawing a sample of the amniotic fluid that envelops the developing human foetus in the uterus. More than 75 abnormalities as well as the sex of the foetus can be ascertained by analysing the foetal cells in amniotic fluid. Perhaps the most common use of the test is to detect Down's syndrome.

Archetype. An archetype is a primeval image, character or pattern that recurs in literature and in thought consistently enough to be considered a universal concept. An archetype is the inherited part of the psyche, inherited from all generations gone before.

Catharsis. (from the Greek katharsis, to cleanse, purge). A purification or purgation of the emotions (*eg* pity and fear) primarily through psychology, fantasy or art. A process that brings about spiritual renewal or release from tension or elimination of a complex by bringing it to consciousness and affording it expression.

Cognition. The act or process of knowing including both awareness and judgment.

Collective unconscious. Those aspects of the psyche that are common to humankind as a whole. Jung's evidence of the collective unconscious is found in myths, legends, folk tales, fairy-tales and dreams.

Complex. A group of associated ideas, repressed desires and memories which have a common, strong emotional tone. These (largely unconscious) ideas exert a dominating influence upon the personality.

Conscious. The content of the mind or mental functioning of which one is aware. It involves perceiving, apprehending or noticing with a degree of controlled thought or observation.

Down's syndrome. Also known as trisomy 21, a common form of mental handicap caused by an abnormality in the chromosomes; formerly known as mongolism, because of the mongoloid features of people with this disorder.

Drama Game. A game in Transactional Analysis in which the three players are identified as Victim, Rescuer and Persecutor.

Ego. One of the three divisions of the psyche in psychoanalytic theory that serves as the organised conscious mediator between the person and reality, especially by functioning both in the perception of and adaptation to reality.

Empathy. The action of understanding, being aware of, being sensitive to, and vicariously experiencing the feelings, thoughts and experience of another of either the past or present without having the feelings, thoughts and experience fully communicated in an objectively explicit manner.

Endocrine system. A series of glands which secrete hormones directly into the blood. It is likened to an orchestra, under the control of the conductor, the pituitary gland in the brain.

Euthanasia. The practice of ending a life so as to release an individual from an incurable disease or intolerable suffering, also called 'mercy killing'. Voluntary euthanasia involves a request by the dying patient or that person's legal representative. Passive or negative euthanasia involves not doing something to prevent death – that is, allowing someone to die; active or positive euthanasia involves taking deliberate action to cause a death.

Frame of reference. A two-part concept which is emphasised in person-centred counselling. The external frame of reference is where we view other people from what something means to us; the internal frame of reference is where we attempt to view what something means to the other person.

Free association. The psychoanalytic technique, whereby the patient reports spontaneous thoughts, ideas or words. The 'golden rule' in psychoanalysis is that the patient reports everything that comes to mind, without any attempt to control or censor it; the unconscious mind is thus tapped. The analyst refrains from any prompt that might influence the patient's selection of material.

Halo effect. The tendency to allow an overall impression of a person or one particular trait to influence the total rating of that person.

Id. One of the three divisions of the psyche in psychoanalytic theory that is completely unconscious and is the source of psychic energy derived from instinctual needs and drives.

Insight. In psychological terms, the discovery by an individual of the psychological connection between earlier and later events so as to lead to recognition of the roots of a particular conflict or conflicts.

Life Positions. A Transactional Analysis term that distinguishes four positions – I'm not OK, You're not OK; I'm not OK, You're OK; I'm OK, You're not OK; I'm OK, You're OK.

Neurosis (or psychoneurosis). An outdated term that describes a variety of psychological disorders having psychic or emotional origins. Not usually severe enough to cause total inability to function in society.

Psyche. In psychology, the centre of thought, feeling and behaviour, which consciously or unconsciously adjusts and relates the body to its social and physical environment.

Psychoanalysis. A theoretical system of psychology based on the work of Sigmund Freud. Psychoanalysis may be defined as human nature interpreted in terms of conflict. The mind is understood as an expression of conflicting forces – some conscious, the majority unconscious.

Psychosynthesis. A synonym for human growth, the ongoing process of integrating all the parts, aspects and energies of the individual into a harmonious, powerful whole. Psychosynthesis draws upon psychoanalysis, Jungian and existential psychology, Buddhism, Yoga and Christian traditions and philosophies.

Resistance. In psychoanalysis, and to some extent in counselling, resistance is opposition to bringing unconscious material into consciousness. It may also be seen in opposing interpretations. In self-counselling, it can be detected by an unwillingness to continue with the process.

Self-actualisation. A person's fundamental tendency towards the fullest realisation of his or her potential. It is a basic concept in humanistic theories of personality, such as those developed by Maslow and Rogers.

Self-determination. The supposed right and practice of a people to achieve self-government, closely related to the concepts of nationalism and the nation-state. When applied to people, it is the person's right to act on the strength of one's personal beliefs and values rather than be coerced by group pressures.

Self-esteem. A confidence and satisfaction in oneself, self-respect.

Stereotypes. Behaviour that classifies groups of people, generally in unfavourable terms. Stereotyping puts people down, because it attributes to them all the characteristics which we have observed in only a few. Stereotyping lumps everybody together; this has come to be known as the halo effect – a tendency to allow an overall impression of a person or one particular outstanding trait to influence the total impression of that person.

Syndrome. A group of signs and symptoms that occur together and characterise a particular abnormality.

Transactional Analysis (TA). A system of analysis and therapy developed by Berne. The theoretical framework comprises: Parent, Adult, Child ego states; transactions between people and between one's various selves; an individual existential position; a preconscious lifeplan or 'script'.

Unconscious. The part of the psychic apparatus that does not ordinarily enter the individual's awareness and that is manifested especially by slips of the tongue or dissociated acts or in dreams. It is a reservoir for data that have never been conscious (primary repression) or that may have been conscious and are later repressed (secondary repression).

Further Reading

A Dictionary of Symbols, J. E. Cirlot (Routledge & Kegan Paul, 1978, reprint).

A-Z of Counselling Theory and Practice, William Stewart (Stanley Thornes, 1997, 2nd edition).

Building Self-Esteem: How To Replace Self-Doubt with Confidence and Well-Being, William Stewart (How To Books, 1998).

Controlling Anxiety: How To Master Your Fears and Phobias and Start Living with Confidence, William Stewart (How To Books, 1998).

Dictionary of Images and Symbols in Counselling, William Stewart (Jessica Kingsley, 1998).

Dictionary for Dreamers, Tom Chetwynd (Paladin, 1984, reprint).

Dictionary of Symbols, Tom Chetwynd (Paladin, 1986, reprint).

'Fairytales and script drama analysis', S. B. Karpman, (1968) *T. A. Bulletin* Vol. 7, (no. 26), April, pp.39–43.

Games People Play, E. Berne (Grove Press, 1964).

Gifts Differing, Isabel Myers Briggs (Consultant Psychologist Press, 1980).

I'm OK – You're OK, Thomas A. Harris (Harper & Row, 1969).

Imagery and Symbolism in Counselling, William Stewart (Jessica Kingsley, 1996).

Interpretation of Dreams, The, Sigmund Freud (Penguin Books, 1991, reprint).

Learning to Counsel: How to Develop the Skills to Work Effectively with Others, Jan Sutton and William Stewart (How To Books, 1997).

Please Understand Me, David Keirsey and Marilyn Bates (Prometheus Nemesis Book, 1984).

Psychology of Consciousness, The, R. E. Ornstein (Pelican, 1975).

Psychosynthesis, Roberto Assagioli (Turnstone Books, 1965).

Self-Analysis, Karen Horney, (W. W. Norton, 1994, reprint).

TA Today, I. Stewart and V. Joines (Lifespace Publishing, 1987).

Thriving on Stress: *How to Manage Pressures and Transform your Life*, Jan Sutton (How To Books, 1997).

Use Both Sides of Your Brain, T. Buzan (E. P. Dutton, 1983).

Other resources

The Institute of Counselling, 6 Dixon Street, Glasgow G1 4AX. In addition to many different distance learning counselling courses, the Institute runs 'An Introduction to Stress Management' and 'Psychology for Counsellors'.

Index

BUILDING SELF-ESTEEM
How to replace self-doubt with confidence and well-being

William Stewart

People who improve their self-esteem find that their lives take on new meaning as confidence grows and well-being is enhanced. This practical, self-help book reveals how the ravages of faulty beliefs about self can be reversed, enabling the reader to develop a firm belief in his or her attributes, accomplishments and abilities. Through a series of exercises and case studies it provides strategies for building self-esteem; it will help readers set clear goals and work steadily towards them. It is also a valuable handbook for those who work in healthcare and counselling. William Stewart is a freelance counsellor, supervisor and author. His background is in nursing, psychiatric social work, and student counselling and lecturing at a London college of nursing.

152pp. illus. 1 85703 251 9.

MAXIMISING YOUR MEMORY
How to train yourself to remember more

Peter Marshall

A powerful memory brings obvious advantages in educational, career and social terms. At school and college those certificates which provide a passport to a career depend heavily on what you can remember in the exam room. In the world of work, being able to recall details which slip the minds of colleagues will give you a competitive edge. In addition, one of the secrets of being popular with customers and friends is to remember their names and the little things which make them feel they matter to you. This book explains clearly how you can maximise your memory in order to achieve your academic, professional and personal goals. Peter Marshall is a member of the Applied Psychology Research Group of the University of London and works primarily on research into superior memory. He recently assisted with the production of Channel 4's *Amazing Memory Show*. He is also author of *How To Study and Learn* in this series.

128pp. illus. 1 85703 234 9.

ACHIEVING PERSONAL WELL-BEING
How to discover and balance your physical and emotional needs

James Chalmers

We tend to shut out natural daylight, work in soulless buildings, expose ourselves to pollution, and live on a diet of junk food. This highly original book is the result of a thorough investigation into how all these factors influence our physical and emotional welfare. It shows how daylight and the environment — including our astrological signs — determine our personality and health, and how by understanding their effects we can take steps towards achieving physical and emotional well-being. The author explores the interrelation of body and mind, and reveals how only by balancing and managing their combined needs can we achieve personal well-being in all aspects of our lives. James Chalmers BSc CEng MIEE is a scientist and an artist. In this book he combines reason and imagination to offer you a remedy for the pressures of modern living.

144pp. illus. 1 85703 272 1.

UNLOCKING YOUR POTENTIAL
How to master your mind, life and destiny

Peter Marshall

Even the smartest individuals will not fulfil their potential on intellect alone; first they must free themselves from their own limiting expectations. If you really want to become master of your own life you will need to remove the barriers to success. This book will show you how to do it. It will introduce you to objective techniques for overcoming the limiting effects of the past: conditioning, misguided or obsolete teachings, repressed conflicts and the expectations imposed on us by others. Peter Marshall is a research psychologist, who specialises in mind and memory, and is a member of the Applied Psychology Research Group of the University of London. He is author of *How To Study and Learn* and *Research Methods* in this series.

144pp. 1 85703 252 7.